BUTTERFLY AND FRIENDS

AN ILLUSTRATED POEM

by

Tamara Martin

Illustrated by:
Sona & Jacob

FIRST EDITION

Little Red Acorns

Printed and bound in the USA

Layout and Cover Design: Michael Linnard, MCSD
Fonts used in this book: Times New Roman, Charlemagne Stad, Arial, Trajan Pro and Gill Sans MT.

First Edition, 2014, manufactured in USA
1 2 3 4 5 6 7 8 9 10 LSI 20 19 18 17 16 15 14

Illustrations: Sona & Jacob

A version of the poem "Butterfly and Friends" first appeared in Sundays in the South, *2006, by Tamara Martin and Vernice Quebodeaux, published by Little Red Tree Publishing.*

Previous books in this collection:

Book 1: The Little Turtle
Book 2: Little Robin Redbreast

Library of Congress Cataloging-in-Publication Data

Martin, Tamara, 1956-
  Butterfly and Friends / written by Tamara Martin, -- 1st ed.
    p. cm.
  ISBN 978-1-935656-32-6 (pbk. : alk. paper)
1. Butterfly--Juvenile poetry. 2. Children's poetry, American. II. Title.
  PS3613.A786235F54 2014
  811'.6--dc22
                    2014958952

Little Red Acorns

An imprint of

Little Red Tree Publishing, LLC
635 Ocean Avenue, New London, CT 06320
website: www.littleredtree.com

For my husband, Michael

For my children, Aimee and Eric

For my granddaughter, Eloise Jolie.

Tamara

Butterfly posed on bended knee

While friends looked on,

Ant and Flea.

"What's wrong, dear butterfly?"

They both asked in despair.

"I've lost my will to live,"

Butterfly said.

"I've completely lost my flair."

"What do you mean?"

Asked Flea, with concern.

"My best friends have left me."

Answered Butterfly, with discern.

"They're just on different paths–

They'll be gone a short while."

Butterfly was relieved

By Ant and Flea's explanation.

He fluttered his wings

With great exaltation.

The moral of this short reprise

Is to understand that

Life is a great surprise.

Wish friends well when

they do go.

They'll be back someday

to continue the show.

BUTTERFLY AND FRIENDS

Butterfly posed on bended knee
While friends looked on, Ant and Flea.

"What's wrong, dear friend?"
They both asked, in despair.

"I've lost my will to live,"
Butterfly said, "I've lost my flair."

"What do you mean?"
Asked Flea with concern.

"My best friends have left me."
Answered Butterfly with discern.

"They're just on different paths—
They'll be gone a short while."

Butterfly was relieved
By his friend's explanation.

He fluttered his wings
With great exaltation.

The moral of this short reprise
Is to understand that
Life is a great surprise.

Wish friends well when they do go.
They'll be back someday
to continue the show.

www.ingramcontent.com/pod-product-compliance
Lightning Source LLC
Chambersburg PA
CBHW041542260326
41914CB00015B/1527

DEMOCRATS versus REPUBLICANS:
Research on the Behaviors of High School Students

First Printing: 2021

LoGiudice Publishing
Orland, IN 46776

Library of Congress Control Number: 2021901977

LOGIUDICE

DEMOCRATS versus REPUBLICANS:

Research on the Behaviors of High School Students

Dawn Larder, Book Editor and Illustrator

LoGiudice Publishing

Orland, IN

Contents

Is There a Difference Between Democrat and Republican States in the Number of Female Students Who Experienced Cyberbullying?

Wayne L. Davis, Ph.D.

Lincoln Memorial University (TN)

Abstract

In the United States, cyberbullying has become a major public health concern. Because there is a difference between the Democrat Party and the Republican Party on their philosophies involving laws and government interventions related to the control of electronic communications, it is important to know if there is a difference between political partisanship and cyberbullying. Data were collected in 2011, 2013, 2015, and 2017 using a three-stage cluster sample design, which produced a nationally representative sample of students in grades 9–12 who attended public and private schools. Initially, this study employed Poisson regression, which is a parametric statistic, in an attempt to answer the research question. However, the model did not adequately fit the data. As a result, another approach was employed using a nonparametric statistic. As an alternative to avoid the distributional assumptions associated with Poisson regression, a generalized estimating equation (GEE) was used. The findings revealed that there was no significant difference between political parties and the percentage of female students who were electronically bullied in their respective jurisdictions.

I. INTRODUCTION

Cyberbullying is the use of electronic or digital media to transmit hostile or aggressive messages with the intent to harm others (Tanrikulu, 2017). Cyberbullying is a major public health concern that may lead to school problems, social problems, and mental health disorders (Hase et al., 2015; Rodríguez-Enríquez et al., 2019). However, cyberspace and electronic information are essential parts of American culture. In the U.S., for example, 95% of teens have access to smartphones and 51% use Facebook (Anderson, 2018; Anderson & Jiang, 2018). About 45% of teens say they are online almost constantly, and 67% of these teens claim to have been cyberbullied. Overall, 60% of girls have experienced at least one abusive online behavior. In short, cyberbullying is a serious problem worthy of study.

U.S. court rulings have made it clear that while hate speech is repulsive, it is protected under the First Amendment unless such speech meets the elements of harassment, it is used to incite a riot, or it contains a direct and credible threat against a person or organization (Banks, 2010; Weaver, 2000). Although there are no federal laws that specifically address cyberbullying, state and local lawmakers have taken action to protect children against cyberbullying (Washington, 2014). In some cases, when bullying overlaps with student harassment, schools are legally obligated to address it. However, schools do not have universal authority in all off-campus cases. In addition, the extent of punishment is controversial. On the one hand, students need to be disciplined for their participation in cyberbullying. On the other hand, students have a constitutional right to freedom of speech.

In the United States, there are two main political parties: Democrats and Republicans. While the Democrats believe in social responsibility and rehabilitation, the Republicans believe in personal responsibility and punishment ("Democrat vs. Republican," n.d.). While Democrats put greater value on communion, Republicans put greater value on agency (Eriksson, 2018). While the Democrats favor government regulations and a more active role of the government in society to protect consumers, the Republicans favor less involvement in terms of roles and responsibilities and oppose government regulations that hinder free market capitalism. These differences in attitudes may have an impact on cyberbullying. Therefore, it is important to know if there is a significant difference between Democrats and Republicans and the amount of cyberbullying in their respective jurisdictions.

The purpose of this study was to determine if there is a difference between political partisanship and the percentage of female students in grades 9-12 who were electronically bullied. The research question and the null hypothesis are listed below.

Research Question: Is there a difference between Democrat and Republican states in the percentage of female students who were electronically bullied?

Null Hypothesis: There is no difference between Democrat and Republican states in the percentage of female students who were electronically bullied.

II. LITERATURE REVIEW

Sylwester and Purver (2015) conducted a qualitative research study to examine the use of language on Twitter accounts between liberals (i.e., Democrats) and conservatives (i.e., Republicans). The researchers used timeline content analysis to analyze the Twitter accounts of 5,373 Democrats and 5,386 Republicans. The findings indicated that Democrats were more likely to use swear words and words that were emotionally expressive. However, there were several limitations in the study. First, the Twitter messages contained noise (i.e., an overwhelming number of apparently unimportant tweets that constantly streamed through the timeline), and some of them may have been run by an institution instead of by an individual. Second, Twitter users may not necessarily be representative of the general population. Finally, the data analysis relied on simple word count and did not consider the actual meanings of the text messages.

Kim et al. (2018) examined the association between cyberbullying and mental health problems. They sampled 31,148 Ontario students in grades 6-12 and used multilevel structural equation modeling to assess the relationships. The findings indicated that cyberbullying was a significant predictor of adolescents' emotional and behavioral problems. However, there were several limitations in this study. First, the students were Canadian and they may not necessarily be representative of American students. Second, the study had a correlational study and cannot determine causal relationships. Finally, because the study was quantitative in nature, it cannot reveal the meanings that participants have given to various phenomena.

Finally, Peng and Davis (2017a; 2017b) conducted a study on political partisanship and cyberbullying in the United States. Data were collected in 2011, 2013, and 2015 using a three-stage cluster sample design, which produced a nationally representative sample of students in grades 9–12 who attended public and private schools. This study employed the independent-samples t-test, and the findings indicated that there was a significant difference in political partisanship and the percentage of female students who were electronically bullied. However, there were several limitations in this study. First, the t-test did not account for the different sample sizes for each state. Second, the study was not an experimental study and cannot determine causal relationships. Finally, because the sample was limited to school students in grades 9-12, the findings cannot be generalized to other populations.

III. METHODOLOGY

Sample
This study examined electronic government-based second-hand data gathered from the Youth Risk

Behavior Surveillance System (YRBSS) in 2011, 2013, 2015, and 2017 (Eaton et al., 2012; Kann et al., 2014; Kann et al., 2016; Kann et al., 2018). The data were collected by the Centers for Disease Control and Prevention, which is devoted to the public's safety and health. A three-stage cluster sample design produced a nationally representative sample of female students in grades 9–12 who attended public and private schools. The standard questionnaire in 2011 and 2013 included 86 questions; the standard questionnaire in 2015 and 2017 included 89 questions. Because the sampling frames for the four surveys were not the same, and it is likely that the students were randomly sampled at the third stage of each study, the data retrieved in 2011, 2013, 2015, and 2017 were initially considered independent.

Z-scores & Poisson Regression

Because the data were presented as percentage values, and each state has a different sample size, a way was needed to take in to account the different sample sizes (Su, 2020). Using a z-score to normalize the data was considered because a z-score is a measure of position that indicates the number of standards deviations a data value lies from the mean. A z-score is a convenient tool when someone wants to compare two variables that are measured in different units. However, contrary to what many people believe, z-scores are not necessarily normally distributed. Although z-scores are linearly transformed scores and have a mean of zero and a standard deviation of one, z-scores follow the exact same distribution as original scores and they do not make the distribution of the data more normal. Thus, it was decided to use Poisson regression because it can use an offset variable to modify each observation so that samples of different sizes can be effectively compared.

Political Partisanship Definition

A state was considered either Democrat or Republican based on the color assigned to that state during U.S. Presidential elections (2008, 2012, and 2016). If a state's electoral college voted for the Democrat U.S. Presidential candidate, then that state was considered a blue state ("Presidential Voting History by State," n.d.). If a state's electoral college voted for the Republican U.S. Presidential candidate, then that state was considered a red state. To be considered in this study, a state had to be consistently red or blue during the years of data collection, which were 2011, 2013, 2015, and 2017.

IV. RESULTS

Although there was a possibility of 200 data values (50 states times four surveys), several states were not considered because they were not consistently red or blue during the data collection period. In addition, several states, which were considered, did not provide cyberbullying data for each of the four surveys. Only the data provided were considered. In short, only 128 data values were considered in this study. See Table 1.

Table 1. **Number of Data Values: 73 Republican Data Values and 55 Democrat Data Values**				
Categorical Variable Information				
			N	Percent
IV = Party	Republican		73	57.0%
	Democrat		55	43.0%
		Total	128	100.0%

The independent-samples t-test was not considered to be the best statistical test to answer the research question because the sample size for each state was different (Su, 2020). The t-test does not take into account the population size of each state, which may produce biased results. However, the Poisson regression will adjust for the population difference for each state by using an offset variable, which will modify each observation so that the count outcome is weighted based on population size. Therefore, to answer the research question, Poisson regression was used with the political party as the predictor variable, the number of bullied females as the outcome variable, and the total number of females for each state as the offset variable.

Table 2. **Descriptive Statistics for the Number of Females Who Were Cyberbullied in the Various States**					
Continuous Variable Information					
	N	Minimum	Maximum	Mean	Std. Deviation
DV = Electronic Bullied: Female	128	68	15867	437.09	1483.641
Offset Variable	128	2.54	4.85	2.9831	.38176

A Poisson distribution assumes that the mean and variance are equal (i.e., a variance to mean ratio of one to one) (Su, 2020). In this case, the mean is 437.09 and the variance, which is the square of the standard deviation, is 2,201,191. This produces a variance to mean ratio of 5,036 to one, which is much larger than a one to one ratio. Thus, there is a large amount of overdispersion, which is problematic.

Deviance goodness-of-fit and Pearson Chi-Square statistics were then used to assess how well the Poisson model fit the data, and the values were 421.932 and 703.870, respectively. A value of one indicates equidispersion (Su, 2020); a value greater than one indicates overdisperson; and a value less than one indicates underdispersion. Thus, the results confirm that there is a large overdisperson problem.

Next, the assumptions of Poisson regression were checked. A Poisson regression model is a generalized linear model and relies on several assumptions (McCullagh & Nelder, 1989).

For a generalized linear model, the following conditions should be satisfied:
1. Independence of each data point
2. Correct distribution of the residuals
3. Correct specification of the variance structure
4. Linear relationship between the response and the linear predictor.

Upon investigation, the independence of observations does not appear to be satisfied. For each state, data were collected over 4 years (2011, 2013, 2015, and 2017). Because data were collected from the same states over multiple years, the observations may not have been independent. The Poisson model did not consider the possible correlation between observations within the same state (Su, 2020).

To check systematic departure from the model, a residual plot that plots residuals against the predicted value of the linear predictor was examined. The null pattern of this plot is a distribution of residuals with mean zero and constant variance (McCullagh & Nelder, 1989; Su, 2020). Typical systematic deviations are the appearance of curvature. Therefore, if the data points are randomly distributed along the 0-horizontal line, it is an indication that the model fitted is adequate for the data. However, the plot displayed an appearance of curvature, which indicates that there is systematic departure from the model and the distribution of the residuals may be problematic.

To check the variance function, a plot of the absolute residuals against fitted values was examined. The null pattern will show no trend, but an ill-chosen variance function will result in a trend in the mean (Su, 2020). Because the scatter plot indicated curvature, it is concluded that the variance function may be inadequate.

Finally, to check if the link function was appropriate, a plot of the predicted values against the actual outcomes was examined. If the link function is appropriate, then the null pattern will be a straight line (Su, 2020). In other words, if the link function is appropriate, the differences between the predicted values and the averaged actual values will be small, and the points will form approximately a straight line. Because the scatter plot of the predicted values and the actual outcomes did not seem to form a straight line, it is concluded that the link function is not appropriate.

In short, the Poisson model did not accurately fit the data. Analyzing non-independent data with techniques that assume independence (ex: generalized linear models) is a widespread practice but one that often produces erroneous results (Aarts et al., 2014; Bakdash & Marusich, 2017; Bland & Altman, 1995;

Su, 2020). Therefore, to answer the research question, a nonparametric statistic was used.

Because the data were not normally distributed, an alternative to avoid distributional assumptions of the response variable (i.e., number of bullied females) leads to a method of estimation that employs a generalized estimating equation (GEE) (Fitzmaurice et al., 2004; Su, 2020). The GEE will describe the model solely in terms of the mean response, the variances, and the pairwise within-subject association. Although GEE is a flexible approach for modeling the mean and the pairwise within-subject association structure, it should be noted that avoidance of distributional assumptions would usually result in some loss of efficiency for the estimation of the coefficients relative to the optimal likelihood-based estimates when distributional assumptions are met.

Below are the results of the parameter estimates for GEE. Even though the data indicate that the rate of being a female victim of cyberbullying is 1.036 times greater for Republican states than for Democrat states, the results are not significant (p = 0.947). In sum, there is no difference between political party and the percentage of female students who were cyberbullied.

Table 3. **The Results of Parameter Estimates Under GEE**											
Parameter Estimates											
			95% Wald Confidence Interval		Hypothesis Test					95% Wald Confidence Interval for Exp(B)	
Parameter	B	Std. Error	Lower	Upper	Wald Chi-Square	df	Sig.	Exp(B)	Lower	Upper
(Intercept)	2.982	.2344	2.522	3.441	161.806	1	.000	19.726	12.459	31.230
[Party=1]	.036	.5305	-1.004	1.075	.005	1	.947	1.036	.366	2.931
[Party=2]	0	.	.	.	.	.	.	1	.	.
(Scale)	1									

Dependent Variable: Electronic Bullied Female
Model: (Intercept), Party, offset = offset

11

V. DISCUSSION

Is there a between Democrat and Republican states in the percentage of female students who were electronically bullied? Although Poisson regression, which is a parametric statistic, was initially thought to be the best statistic for answering the research question, it was determined to be less than optimal when its assumptions were checked, which occurred after the data were collected. As a result, a nonparametric statistic, GEE, was used to answer the research question. Although GEE is more flexible than Poisson regression because it does not rely on the Poisson regression's assumptions, there is a loss of efficiency for the estimation of the coefficients (Fitzmaurice et al., 2004; Su, 2020). In other words, nonparametric statistics are not as strong as parametric statistics (Field, 2005).

The results of the GEE test indicate that there is no statistically significant difference between Democrat and Republican states in the percentage of female students who were electronically bullied. The results are important because an earlier research study based on the independent-samples t-test indicated that female students in Democrat states were less likely to be cyberbullied than female students in Republican states (Peng & Davis, 2017a). Although the Democrat Party and the Republican Party have different philosophies on government regulations and responsibilities, neither philosophy seems to better than the other involving the number of female students who have been cyberbullied. This study may spark interest into developing better strategies for reducing cyberbullying. It indicates the need for additional research.

There were several limitations in this study. First, because the sample was limited to female students in grades 9-12, the findings cannot be generalized to other populations (Champion, 2006). Second, it is not possible to know the actual number of victims because many violations go unreported (Berry & Smith, 2000; U.S. Department of Justice, 2010). Third, because cyberbullying is a recent issue, there were only four youth risk behavior surveillance surveys of available data. Thus, the amount of data available is less than optimal. Fourth, because the data used in the study were second-hand and collected for a different reason, the data values cannot be more clearly defined. Finally, because the study was quantitative in nature, it does not provide an in-depth understanding of the meanings that the participants have associated with their lived experiences (Berg, 2007).

REFERENCES

Aarts, E., Verhage, M., Veenvliet, J. V., Dolan, C. V., & van der Sluis, S. (2014). A solution to dependency: using multilevel analysis to accommodate nested data. *Nature Neuroscience, 17*, 491–496.

Anderson, M. (2018). *A majority of teens have experienced some form of cyberbullying.* https://www.pewresearch.org/internet/2018/09/27/a-majority-of-teens-have-experienced-some-form-of-cyberbullying/

Anderson, M., & Jiang, J. (2018). *Teens, Social Media & Technology 2018.* https://www.pewresearch.org/internet/2018/05/31/teens-social-media-technology-2018/

Bakdash, J. Z., & Marusich, L. R. (2017). Repeated measures correlation. *Frontiers in Psychology, 8, 456.*

Banks, J, (2010). Regulating hate speech online. *International Review of Law, Computers & Technology,* 24(3), 233 –239.

Berg, B. (2007). *Qualitative research methods for the social sciences* (6th ed.). Boston, MA: Pearson Education, Inc.

Berry, B., & Smith, E. (2000). Race, sport, and crime: The misrepresentation of African Americans in team sports and crime. *Sociology of Sport Journal, 17*(2), 171-197.

Bland, J. M , & Altman, D. G. (1995). Calculating correlation coefficients with repeated observations: Part 2—Correlation between subjects. *BMJ, 310*(6980), 633.

Champion, D. (2006). *Research methods for criminal justice and criminology* (3rd ed.). Upper Saddle River, NJ: Pearson Merrill Prentice Hall.

Democrat vs. Republican (n.d.). https://www.diffen.com/difference/Democrat_vs_Republican

Eaton, D.K., Kann, L., Kinchen, S., Shanklin, S., Flint, K.H., Hawkins, . . . Whittle, L. (2012). Youth risk behavior surveillance—United States, 2011. *Morbidity and Mortality Weekly Report: Surveillance Summaries, 61*(4), 1-162. https://www.cdc.gov/mmwr/pdf/ss/ss6104.pdf

Eriksson, K. (2018). Republicans value agency, Democrats value communion. *Social Psychology Quarterly, 81*(2) 173–184.

Field, A. (2005). *Discovering statistics using SPSS* (2nd ed.). Thousand Oaks, CA: Sage.

Fitzmaurice, G. M., Laird, N. M., & Ware, J. H. (2004). *Applied longitudinal analysis.* Hoboken, NJ: John Wiley & Sons.

Hase, C.N., Goldberg, S.B., Smith, D., Stuck, A., & Campaign, J. (2015). Impacts of traditional bullying and cyberbullying on the mental health of middle school and high school students. *Psychology in the Schools, 52*(6), 607-617.

Kann, L., Kinchen, S., Shanklin, S.L., Flint, K.H., Hawkins, J., Harris, W.A., . . . Zaza, S. (2014). Youth risk behavior surveillance—United States, 2013. *Morbidity and Mortality Weekly Report: Surveillance Summaries, 63*(4), 1-172. https://www.cdc.gov/mmwr/pdf/ss/ss6304.pdf

Kann, L., McManus, T., Harris, W.A., Shanklin, S.L., Flint, K.H., Hawkins, . . . Zaza, S. (2016). Youth risk behavior surveillance—United States, 2015. *Morbidity and Mortality Weekly Report: Surveillance Summaries, 65*(6), 1-180. https://www.cdc.gov/healthyyouth/data/yrbs/pdf/2015/ss6506_updated.pdf

Kann, L., McManus, T., Harris, W.A., Shanklin, S.L., Flint, K.H., Hawkins, J., Queen, B., . . . Ethier, K.A. (2018). Youth risk behavior surveillance—United States, 2017. *Morbidity and Mortality Weekly Report: Surveillance Summaries, 67*(8), 1-479. https://www.cdc.gov/healthyyouth/data/yrbs/pdf/2017/ss6708.pdf

Kim, S., Colwell, S.R., Kata, A., Boyle, M.H., & Georgiades, K. (2018). Cyberbullying victimization and adolescent mental health: Evidence of differential effects by sex and mental health problem type. *Journal of Youth and Adolescence, 47,* 661-672. doi: 10.1007/s10964-017-0678-4

McCullagh, P., & Nelder, J. A. (1989). Generalized linear models. Cambridge: University Press.

Peng, Y., & Davis, W. (2017a). Partisanship and cyberbullying in the United States. *Asian Academic Research Journal of Social Science & Humanities, 4*(7), 133-139.

Peng, Y., & Davis, W. (2017b). *Partisanship, cyberbullying, & suicidal thoughts.* Bloomington, IN: Xlibris.

Presidential voting history by state (n.d.). https://ballotpedia.org/Presidential_voting_history_by_state

Rodríguez-Enríquez, M., Bennasar-Veny, M., Leiva, A., Garaigordobil, M., & Yañez, A.M. (2019). *BMC Public Health, 19*(1), 1-7.

Su, Y. (2020). *Dr. Su Statistics.* https://sites.google.com/site/drsustat/

Sylwester K. & Purver M. (2015). *Twitter language use reflects psychological differences between Democrats and Republicans.* doi: 10.1371/journal.pone.01137422.

Tanrikulu, I. (2017). Cyberbullying prevention and intervention programs in schools: A systematic review. *School Psychology International, 2018,* 74–91.

U.S. Department of Justice, Office of Justice Programs, Bureau of Justice Statistics (2010). *Criminal victimization in the United States, 2007 statistical tables: National crime victimization survey.* http://bjs.ojp.usdoj.gov/content/pub/pdf/cvus0705.pdf

Washington, E.T. (2014). An overview of cyberbullying in higher education. *Adult Learning, 26*(1), 21-27.

Weaver, R.L. (2000). Free speech, crime, and the challenge of advancing technology. *International Review of Law, Computers & Technology, 14*(1), 25-32.

Is There a Relationship Between the Number of Female Students Who Were Cyberbullied and the Number of Female Students Who Seriously Considered Attempting Suicide?

Wayne L. Davis, Ph.D.

Lincoln Memorial University (TN)

Abstract

In the United States, cyberbullying has become a major public health concern. Indeed, many people who are victims of cyberbullying consider harming themselves. Because criminal justice practitioners are concerned with public safety, this is an area worthy of study. The general purpose of this study was to investigate whether there is a correlation between the percentage of female students who were electronically bullied and the percentage of female students who seriously considered suicide. Data were collected in 2011, 2013, 2015, and 2017 using a three-stage cluster sample design, which produced a nationally representative sample of female students in grades 9–12 who attended public and private schools. As an alternative to avoid the distributional assumptions of independent observations, this study used a generalized estimating equation (GEE). The findings revealed that there was no significant difference between the percentage of female students who were electronically bullied and the percentage of female students who seriously considered suicide.

I. INTRODUCTION

Cyberbullying is the use of electronic or digital media to harass, humiliate, or threaten another person (Holladay, 2010). Cyberbullying is different than face-to-face bullying because electronic communications allow cyberbullies to maintain anonymity, and perpetrators can communicate messages to large audiences very quickly (Schneider et al., 2012). Although individuals may not want to engage in face-to-face bullying, they may be enticed to engage in cyberbullying because they may feel reduced responsibility and accountability. This is a major problem because 71% of American youth use Facebook, 52% use Instagram, 41% use Snapchat, and 33% use Twitter (Lenhart, 2015). Ninety-two percent of American youth have stated that they go online daily, and 24% of them have stated that they are online constantly. Cyberbullying is a major public health concern because it has been linked to school problems, social problems, mental health disorders, and suicide (Hase et al., 2015; Rodríguez-Enríquez et al., 2019; Wood, 2018).

Hundreds of thousands of individuals have experienced cyberbullying, and many of them have experienced it for more than one year (Evans, 2012). Youths who experience cyberbullying are more than twice as likely to hurt themselves or to attempt suicide (Wood, 2018). Thus, cyberbullying is a major social problem that is worthy of study. This correlational study will add to the body of knowledge by examining data that were collected by the Centers for Disease Control and Prevention. The research question and the null hypothesis are listed below.

Research Question: Is there a relationship between the percentage of female students who were cyberbullied and the percentage of female students who seriously considered attempting suicide?

Null Hypothesis: There is no relationship between the percentage of female students who were cyberbullied and the percentage of female students who seriously considered attempting suicide.

II. LITERATURE REVIEW

John et al. (2018) conducted a meta study on 33 articles from 26 independent studies to determine the relationship between cyberbullying and self-harm or suicidal behaviors in individuals younger than 25 years of age. A major benefit of a meta-analysis is that it provides a quantitative analysis of a large, consolidated body of literature (Haidich, 2010). Using odds ratios as a summary measure of effect size, the findings indicated that, compared with nonvictims, those who experienced cyberbullying were 235% more likely to harm themselves and 257% more likely to attempt suicide (John et al., 2018). In short, victims of cyberbullying were at a greater risk than nonvictims of intentionally hurting themselves.

However, there were several limitations in the John et. al (2018) study. First, because a meta-analysis examines aggregates of data, the relationship between being a victim of cyberbullying and engaging in self-harm for any particular person cannot be determined. Second, a failure to include a majority of existing studies can lead to wrong conclusions (Lee, 2019). Because research studies that do not reject null hypotheses tend to remain unpublished, there may be a bias toward using studies with positive results. This will compromise the validity of a meta-analysis. Fourth, a meta-analysis relies on shared subjectivity when deciding how similar studies should be combined. Indeed, every form of analysis requires certain subjective decisions. Finally, quantitative studies do not provide an in-depth understanding of the meanings that the participants have associated with their lived experiences (Berg, 2007).

Hinduja and Patchin (2010) surveyed 1,963 middle school students from one school district in the United States to assess the relationship between cyberbullying and suicide ideation. The students were surveyed on their Internet use and experiences. Respondents were asked about their experiences with bullying and peer harassment, both online and offline, and thoughts about committing suicide. The researchers utilized logistic regression analysis and found that being a victim of cyberbullying is associated with an increase in suicidal ideation.

However, the Hinduja and Patchin (2010) study has several limitations. First, because the data were not collected over time, it is impossible to determine the proper temporal ordering among the variables. Second, the participants may have engaged in acquiescence bias by simply selecting positive responses over negative responses. Third, recall bias may have occurred due to individuals misrepresenting or distorting facts from previous time periods. Fourth, because the students who were surveyed attended only one school district, they may not necessarily be representative of other populations across the country.

Peng et al. (2019) conducted a study to determine if being the victim of cyberbullying is related to self-harm and suicide attempts. The researchers used a sample of 2,647 Chinese students from 10 junior high schools. Data for self-harm and suicide attempts were collected using a self-administered survey. The psychopathy of each student was assessed using the Strengths and Difficulties Questionnaire. Using multinomial logistic regression, the findings indicated that, compared to nonvictims, victims of cyberbullying were at a greater risk of harming themselves and attempting suicide.

However, the Peng et al. (2019) study has several limitations. First, although the study determined correlational relationships, the study did not indicate causal relationships. Second, because the study was quantitative in nature, it cannot reveal the meanings that participants have given to various phenomena (Berg, 2007). Finally, the sample consisted of Chinese students who may be different than American students in a meaningful way (Peng et al., 2019). As a result, the study's findings may not be generalized to other populations that do not match the sample's characteristics.

Peng and Davis (2017a; 2017b) conducted a study to investigate the correlation between the percentage of students who were electronically bullied and the percentage of students who seriously considered suicide. Data were collected in 2011, 2013, and 2015 using a three-stage cluster sample design, which produced a nationally representative sample of students in grades 9–12 who attended public and private schools. The researchers employed linear regression analysis and the findings indicated that once female students were cyberbullied, they seriously considered suicide.

However, the Peng and Davis (2017a; 2017b) study has several limitations. First, the study was not an experimental study and cannot determine causal relationships. Second, because the sample was limited to American students in grades 9-12 in public and private schools, the findings cannot be generalized to other populations. Finally, linear regression assumes that the observations were independent, which may be a problem because data in the study were collected multiple times from the same states (Norusis, 2008; Su, 2020).

Kyriacou and Issitt (2018) explored the perceptions of student teachers regarding cyberbullying by students against other students. Data were collected from 97 secondary student teachers at a university in England who were mostly in their early 20s and who attended high school when cyberbullying was becoming common. The sample consisted of 41 males, 54 females, and two who did not indicate their sex. The participants were provided a questionnaire that asked them to express their views about the motives behind cyberbullying and about the actions that can be implemented to deal with the problem. Most of the questions on the survey used a Likert-type scale. Based on mean scores and on one open-ended question, the findings indicated that student teachers believe that cyberbullying can be reduced through education on e-safety and by implementing heavy sanctions against perpetrators.

However, the Kyriacou and Issitt (2018) study has several limitations. First, because the study was qualitative in nature, it failed to provide patterns of relationships through numerical representations. Second, the participants were student teachers who lived in England, and they may not necessarily reflect the opinions of seasoned teachers in America. Third, because Likert-type scales were used, there is the possibility that the participants a) committed central tendency bias by simply selecting the middle option rather than the best option, b) committed acquiescence bias by simply selecting positive responses over negative responses, or c) were forced to select options that did not accurately represent their realities (Antonovich, 2008). Finally, the sample consisted of student teachers who, compared to seasoned teachers, may not be fully aware of the variety of resources available at educational institutions.

Finally, Paul et al. (2012) investigated the students' perceived effectiveness of coping strategies and school interventions related to traditional bullying and cyberbullying. A sample of 217 students, which consisted of 118 males and 99 females in grades 7-9, completed a worksheet on coping strategies. A sample of 190 students, which consisted of 95 males and 95 females in grades 7-9, evaluated school interventions. The worksheets used to collect data were designed to measure student perception of different coping strategies and school interventions related to traditional bullying and cyberbullying. The analysis of the item ratings was conducted using the Wilcoxon signed ranks test. In addition, comparisons between item ratings and participant role type (i.e., victim, bully, or no role) were conducted using the Kruskall-Wallis test and the Mann-Whitney U post-hoc test. Although the students felt that seeking help and advice were effective coping mechanisms, and that school sanctions, informal approach, and support approach were effective intervention mechanisms, the findings indicated that the most helpful approach requires the support of family members, especially the parents.

However, the Paul et al. (2012) study has several limitations. First, the findings cannot necessarily be generalized to other individuals who do not match the sample's characteristics. Second, because the application of anti-bullying interventions is unique to each school, it is important to exercise caution in drawing conclusions. Finally, the coping skills adopted by each student might be influenced by the atmosphere of the student's particular environment.

III. METHODOLOGY

Sample
This study examined electronic government-based second-hand data gathered from the Youth Risk Behavior Surveillance System (YRBSS) in 2011, 2013, 2015, and 2017 (Eaton et al., 2012; Kann et al., 2014; Kann et al., 2016; Kann et al., 2018). The data were collected by the Centers for Disease Control and Prevention, which is devoted to the public's safety and health. A three-stage cluster sample design produced a nationally representative sample of students in grades 9–12 who attended public and private schools. The standard questionnaire in 2011 and 2013 included 86 questions; the standard questionnaire in 2015 and 2017 included 89 questions.

Statistical Analysis
Because the observations for the four questionnaires used in 2011, 2013, 2015, and 2017 were from the same states, a certain amount of correlation/dependence was expected (Su, 2020). Indeed, a prior study that used Poisson regression on data from the same surveys over the same time period has indicated that the data values have a very large overdisperson problem (a variance to mean ratio of 5,036 to one) (Davis, 2020). Thus, in order to address this overdispersion problem, a generalized estimating equation (GEE), which is a nonparametric statistic, was used in the current study to assess the relationship between the number of females who were cyberbullied and the number of females who seriously considered suicide. Although GEE avoids the distributional assumptions of independent observations, the use of a

nonparametric statistic would usually result in some loss of efficiency for the estimation of the coefficients relative to the optimal likelihood-based estimates when distributional assumptions are satisfied (Fitzmaurice et al., 2004; Su, 2020).

IV. RESULTS

GEE was used to assess the relationship between the number of females who were cyberbullied (i.e., predictor variable) and the number of females who seriously considered suicide (i.e., outcome variable). The findings indicate that there is no relationship between the predictor variable and the outcome variable (p = 0.625). Therefore, the null hypothesis was accepted.

Table 1. **The Results of Parameter Estimates Under GEE**										
Parameter Estimates										
			95% Wald Confidence Interval		Hypothesis Test				95% Wald Confidence Interval for Exp(B)	
Parameter	B	Std. Error	Lower	Upper	Wald Chi-Square	df	Sig.	Exp(B)	Lower	Upper
(Intercept)	-1.330	.1771	-1.677	-.983	56.441	1	.000	.264	.187	.374
Female Cyberbully Rate	-.435	.8905	-2.180	1.310	.239	1	.625	.647	.113	3.707
(Scale)	1									

Events: Female Suicide Rate

Trials: Female Sample Size

Model: (Intercept), Female Cyberbully Rate

V. DISCUSSION

The results of the GEE assessment indicate that there is no statistically significant relationship between the number of females who were cyberbullied and the number of females who seriously considered suicide. The results are important because an earlier research study conducted by Peng and Davis (2017a) used much of the same data, and their findings indicated that female students who were cyberbullied were more likely to have seriously considered suicide. However, unlike the current study, Peng and Davis assumed that the observations were independent. When the observations were not considered independent, female students who were cyberbullied were not more likely to have seriously considered suicide. This study is important because it shows the importance of assumptions, and how those assumptions can impact the findings.

Limitations

There were several limitations in this study. First, because the sample was limited to female students in grades 9-12, the findings cannot be generalized to other populations. Second, it is not possible to know the actual number of victims because many students who are bullied never officially report it to authorities (Loveless, 2020). Third, because cyberbullying is a recent issue, there were only four youth risk behavior surveillance surveys of available data. Thus, the amount of data available is less than optimal. Fourth, because the data used in the study were second-hand and collected for a different reason, the data values cannot be more clearly defined. Finally, because the study was quantitative in nature, it does not provide an in-depth understanding of the meanings that the participants have associated with their lived experiences (Berg, 2007).

Further Research

Following are ideas for additional research. First, to eliminate the problem of using different sample sizes from each state, a researcher could collect original data using a fixed sample size from each state. In addition, if the data were collected at one point in time, then the researcher could ensure that the data values are independent. By doing this, the researcher may be able to use a parametric statistic to assess the relationship between cyberbullying and serious suicidal thoughts. For example, although GEE is more flexible than Poisson regression because it does not rely on the Poisson regression's assumptions, there is a loss of efficiency for the estimation of the coefficients when a nonparametric statistic is used (Fitzmaurice et al., 2004; Su, 2020). In other words, nonparametric statistics are not as strong as parametric statistics (Field, 2005). Second, even if a study indicates that there is a relationship between being cyberbullied and seriously considering suicide, it will not indicate why individuals seriously consider suicide. A qualitative study needs to be performed to address the reasons why individuals seriously consider suicide. Finally, variables that are believed to reduce cyberbullying can be studied, which will be based on specific theories. If a theory effectively explains the problem, then the same theory can be used to resolve the problem. To do this, data must be collected in a manner that is in alignment with the theory of interest. For example, if it is believed that the deterrence theory can be used to reduce cyberbullying, then data on deterrence and cyberbullying need to be collected. If the fear of punishment is quantified and is shown to be inversely related to the amount cyberbullying, then a resolution based on the celerity, certainty, and severity of punishment can be implemented to address the problem (Barkan, 2006).

REFERENCES

Antonovich, M.P. (2008). *Office and SharePoint 2007 user's guide: Integrating SharePoint with Excel, Outlook, Access, and Word*. Berkeley, CA: Apress.

Barkan, S. (2006). *Criminology: A sociological understanding* (3rd ed.). Upper Saddle River, NJ: Pearson Prentice Hall.

Berg, B. (2007). *Qualitative research methods for the social sciences* (6th ed.). Boston, MA: Pearson Education, Inc.

Davis, W.L. (2020). Is There a Difference Between Democrat and Republican States in the Number of Female Students Who Experienced Cyberbullying? *Lincoln Memorial Journal of Social Sciences, 1*(1), Article 1.

Eaton, D.K., Kann, L., Kinchen, S., Shanklin, S., Flint, K.H., Hawkins, . . . Whittle, L. (2012). Youth risk behavior surveillance—United States, 2011. *Morbidity and Mortality Weekly Report: Surveillance Summaries, 61*(4), 1-162. https://www.cdc.gov/mmwr/pdf/ss/ss6104.pdf

Evans, G. (2012). Cyberbullying leaves its victims close to suicide (features). *Western Mail (Cardiff, Wales), 6,* 6.

Field, A. (2005). *Discovering statistics using SPSS* (2nd ed.). Thousand Oaks, CA: Sage.

Fitzmaurice, G. M., Laird, N. M., & Ware, J. H. (2004). *Applied longitudinal analysis*. Hoboken, NJ: John Wiley & Sons.

Haidich, A.B. (2010). Meta-analysis in medical research. *Hippokratia: Quarterly Medical Journal, 14*(1), 29-37.

Hase, C.N., Goldberg, S.B., Smith, D., Stuck, A., & Campaign, J. (2015). Impacts of traditional bullying and cyberbullying on the mental health of middle school and high school students. *Psychology in the Schools, 52*(6), 607-617.

Hinduja, S., & Patchin, J.W. (2010). Bullying, cyberbullying, and suicide. *Archives of Suicide Research, 14,* 206-221. doi: 10.1080/13811118.2010.494133

Holladay, J. (2010). Cyberbullying: The stakes have never been higher for students – or schools. *Teaching Tolerance*, 38. https://www.tolerance.org/magazine/fall-2010/cyberbullying

John, A., Glendenning A.C., Marchant, A., Montgomery, P. Stewart, A., Wood, S., Lloyd, K., Hawton, K. (2018). Self-Harm, Suicidal Behaviours, and Cyberbullying in Children and Young People: Systematic Review. *Journal of Medical Internet Research, 20*(4), e129. doi: 10.2196/jmir.9044

Kann, L., Kinchen, S., Shanklin, S.L., Flint, K.H., Hawkins, J., Harris, W.A., . . . Zaza, S. (2014). Youth risk behavior surveillance—United States, 2013. *Morbidity and Mortality Weekly Report: Surveillance Summaries, 63*(4), 1-172. https://www.cdc.gov/mmwr/pdf/ss/ss6304.pdf

Kann, L., McManus, T., Harris, W.A., Shanklin, S.L., Flint, K.H., Hawkins, . . . Zaza, S. (2016). Youth risk behavior surveillance—United States, 2015. *Morbidity and Mortality Weekly Report: Surveillance Summaries, 65*(6), 1-180. https://www.cdc.gov/healthyyouth/data/yrbs/pdf/2015/ss6506_updated.pdf

Kann, L., McManus, T., Harris, W.A., Shanklin, S.L., Flint, K.H., Hawkins, J., Queen, B., . . . Ethier,

K.A. (2018). Youth risk behavior surveillance—United States, 2017. *Morbidity and Mortality Weekly Report: Surveillance Summaries, 67*(8), 1-479. https://www.cdc.gov/healthyyouth/data/yrbs/pdf/2017/ss6708.pdf

Kyriacou, C., & Issitt, J. (2018). Student teachers' perceptions of cyberbullying in schools. *The Psychology of Education Review, 42*(2), 23-27.

Lee, Y.H. (2019). Strengths and Limitations of Meta-Analysis. *The Korean Journal of Medicine, 94*(5), 391-395.

Lenhart, A. (2015). Teens, social media & technology overview 2015. *Pew Research Center.* http://www.pewinternet.org/2015/04/09/teens-social-media-technology-2015/

Loveless, B. (2020). *Bullying Epidemic: Facts, Statistics and Prevention.* https://www.educationcorner.com/bullying-facts-statistics-and-prevention.html

Norusis, M.J. (2008). *SPSS 16.0 guide to data analysis.* Upper saddle River, NJ: Prentice Hall.

Paul, S., Smith, P.K., Blumberg, H.H. (2012). Comparing student perceptions of coping strategies and school interventions in managing bullying and cyberbullying incidents. *Pastoral Care in Education, 30*(2), 127-146.

Peng, Y., & Davis, W. (2017a). Cyberbullying & suicidal thoughts in the United States. *Asian Academic Research Journal of Social Science & Humanities, 4*(7), 102-109.

Peng, Y., & Davis, W. (2017b). *Partisanship, cyberbullying, & suicidal thoughts.* Bloomington, IN: Xlibris.

Peng, Z., Klomek, A.B., Li, L., Su, X., Sillanmaki, L., Chudal, R., & Sourander, A. (2019). Associations between Chinese adolescents subjected to traditional and cyber bullying and suicide ideation, self-harm and suicide attempts. *BMC Psychiatry, 19*, 324. https://doi.org/10.1186/s12888-019-2319-9

Rodríguez-Enríquez, M., Bennasar-Veny, M., Leiva, A., Garaigordobil, M., & Yañez, A.M. (2019). *BMC Public Health, 19*(1), 1-7.

Schneider, S.K., O'Donnell, L., Stueve, A., & Coulter, R.W.S. (2012). Cyberbullying, school bullying, and psychological distress: A regional census of high school students. *American Journal of Public Health, 102*(1), 171-177.

Su, Y. (2020). *Dr. Su Statistics.* https://sites.google.com/site/drsustat/

Wood, J. (2018). Cyberbullying Victims May Be Twice as Likely to Self-Harm and Show Suicidal Behaviors. *Psych Central.* https://psychcentral.com/news/2018/04/22/cyberbullying-victims-may-be-twice-as-likely-to-self-harm-and-show-suicidal-behaviors/134780.html

Political Partisanship and Male High School Students Who Have Used Marijuana

Jordan Caldwell, Lincoln Memorial University (TN)
&
Wayne L. Davis, Ph.D., Columbia College (SC)

Abstract

There are opposing viewpoints on whether marijuana should be legalized. Democrats and Republicans have different attitudes toward the drug. Democrats believe marijuana should be legalized for medical patients, if it is prescribed by a physician and is needed to reduce severe pain. In addition, Democrats believe that the war on recreational marijuana has been a waste of time and government resources. Many Democrats are in favor of legalizing recreational marijuana because it is considered normal by social standards. Republicans, on the other hand, oppose legalizing medical marijuana because they believe other drugs can be prescribed by physicians to reduce pain experienced by medical patients. In addition, Republicans believe that legalizing medical marijuana will lead to legalizing recreational marijuana, which is dangerous and a threat to public safety and health. According to Akers' social learning theory, individuals learn behaviors according to the frequency, importance, intensity, and duration of the social learning experiences. Children will learn how to act through communications with intimate others, by definitions defined as favorable by others, and by observing how other individuals are rewarded and punished. Because public safety and children's health are important social issues, and the government controls society, it is important to know if the behaviors of high school students are being affected by the different social learning environments created by the government. The researchers examined electronic second-hand data on marijuana use, which were collected in 2013, 2015, and 2017 by the Centers for Disease Control and Prevention. The results of logistic regression for repeated measures indicate that there is no statistically significant relationship between male high school students who have ever used marijuana and political party.

I. INTRODUCTION

Many Americans smoke marijuana and/or consume marijuana products (Foundation for a Drug-Free World, 2020). For example, over 94 million Americans have admitted using marijuana at least once, 2.1 million Americans admitted abusing marijuana, and 6.7% of marijuana users are children who are 12 to 17 years of age. Marijuana is readily available in America, and domestic marijuana production has increased from 2.2 million pounds to 22 million pounds over the last 25 years.

Some individuals argue that marijuana is harmful. First, marijuana has over 400 chemicals in it, it produces 2,000 chemicals when smoked, it contains cancer causing chemicals, and it is much more harmful than alcohol (Califano, 1998; Stimson, 2012). Second, marijuana can damage the lungs, brain, and bones because it is toxic (Porter, 2012). Third, smoking marijuana adversely affects the immune system and it contributes to chronic coughing, respiratory diseases, and leukemia (Fanning, 2011). Fourth, marijuana is addicting and more than 2,500 youths each year require emergency room services, which are overtaxing the emergency rooms (Burns, 2006; Walters, 2005). Fifth, if marijuana is illegal, then the courts can formally order the addicted youths to receive the necessary treatment, which can then be monitored by the authorities (Moline,1998). Finally, some research has shown that early marijuana use negatively affects educational outcomes and it is positively related to aggression and crime (Cobb-Clark et al., 2015; Odgers et al., 2008).

Some individuals argue that marijuana may be beneficial. First, preclinical data have demonstrated that cannabinoids may spur brain cell growth (Armentano, 2012). Second, marijuana is neuroprotective and protects against alcohol-induced brain damage. For example, the administration of marijuana has reduced ethanol-induced brain cell death by up to 60%. Third, cancerous glioma tumors, which typically do not respond to standard medical treatments, do response to cannabis. Marijuana has been shown to target malignant cells while ignoring healthy ones. Fourth, there is evidence that marijuana slows the progression of certain neurodegenerative diseases, such as Parkinson's disease and Multiple Sclerosis. Fifth, research has indicated that most of the crime committed by juveniles involve possessing and using marijuana, and that there was no relationship between non-drug specific charges and marijuana use (Pedersen & Skardhamar, 2009). Finally, users of marijuana agreed that marijuana has therapeutic benefits in treating depression, painful conditions, anxiety, and insomnia (Keyhani, 2018).

There are opposing viewpoints on whether marijuana should be legalized. Democrats and Republicans have different attitudes toward the drug (Snyder, 2016). Democrats believe marijuana should be legalized for medical patients, if it is prescribed by a physician and is needed to reduce severe pain. In addition, Democrats believe that the war on recreational marijuana has been a waste of time and government resources. Many Democrats are in favor of legalizing recreational marijuana because it is considered normal by social standards. Republicans, on the other hand, oppose legalizing medical marijuana because they believe other drugs can be prescribed by physicians to reduce pain experienced by medical patients. In addition Republicans believe that legalizing medical marijuana will lead to legalizing recreational marijuana, which is dangerous and a threat to public safety and health. In 2005, for example, there were 242,200 emergency room visits across the country (for youths and adults), which involved the use of marijuana (Foundation for a Drug-Free World, 2020).

According to Akers' social learning theory, individuals learn to behave according to the frequency, importance, intensity, and duration of their social learning experiences (Akers & Sellers, 2009). Children will learn how to act through communications with intimate others, by definitions defined as favorable by others, and by observing how other individuals are rewarded and punished. In addition, role modeling occurs in early childhood, when humans are at their greatest developmental rate for learning. This is important because parents, teachers, and other individuals in the social environment can have a strong lifelong influence on children's behaviors. For example, if marijuana becomes readily available and its use is deemed acceptable by significant others, then it is expected that more high school students will learn to use marijuana. Indeed, according to a study by Keyes et al. (2011), there is a positive relationship between the approval of marijuana use from a person's birth cohort and the individual's use of marijuana, independent of the person's personal attitude toward marijuana use.

Because the use of marijuana is a political issue, and the government controls society, it is important to know if the behaviors of high school students are being affected by the different social learning environments created by the government. Because public safety and children's health are important social issues, it is important to know if there is a difference in the number of children who use marijuana in the two different social learning environments. Thus, the purpose of this study was to determine if there is a difference between political partisanship and the percentage of male high school students who have ever used marijuana. The research question and the null hypothesis are listed below.

Research Question: Is there a difference between Democrat and Republican states in the percentage of male high school students who have ever used marijuana?

Null Hypothesis: There is no difference between Democrat and Republican states in the percentage of male high school students who have ever used marijuana.

II. LITERATURE REVIEW

First, Eisenberg et al. (2019) conducted a qualitative study to examine the marijuana-related attitudes, behaviors, and challenges of parents involving the legalization of marijuana. The researchers collected data from 54 parents in Seattle via six focus groups. A structured interview protocol was used to ask the participants about their parenting behaviors in a marijuana-legal environment. The researchers used NVivo software to perform content analysis. The findings indicate that, although most parents did not approve of their children consuming marijuana, they expected it would happen. Therefore, the parents indicated that they talked with their children about the drug and its effect, and the parents set marijuana-consuming guidelines in their homes. However, several parents found it hard to monitor their children's behaviors and difficult to discuss their own personal use of the drug. Parents stated that they needed to learn how to better deal with the situation by attending programs that teach strategies on how to deal with the situation. Thus, the parents believe that the social learning environment (i.e., training classes) will modify their behaviors.

However, there were several limitations in the Eisenberg et al. (2019) study. First, the sample was comprised of parents in the Seattle area who are believed to have very permissive views toward the use of marijuana, and they may not necessarily reflect parents in other areas outside Seattle. Second, the sample consisted of college graduates and may not necessarily represent parents with different educational and socioeconomic backgrounds who may face different challenges. Third, individuals who were invited to participate in the study, but who had fewer concerns about marijuana, may have declined to participate. As a result, the findings may be biased. Finally, qualitative studies do not quantify relationships, identify patterns, or make numeric predictions (Bordens & Abbott, 2008).

Second, Verweij et al. (2010) conducted a meta-analysis study to determine the magnitude of environmental influences on marijuana use. The researchers examined 52 existing twin studies from western countries. The researchers meta-analyzed the standardized variance components for initiation of cannabis use and problematic cannabis use by calculating the weighted average for shared and unshared environmental estimates. The findings indicated that there is a relationship between siblings, friends, and peers and the abuse of cannabis in young adults.

However, there were several limitations in the Verweij et al. (2010) study. First, the findings, which were based on studies of twins, may not necessarily be generalized to the general population. Second, the 52 twin studies differed in their measures, their statistical methods, and the characteristics of their samples. Finally, because the study was quantitative in nature, it does not provide an in-depth understanding of the motives behind the actions of the participants (Berg, 2007).

Third, Willis et al. (2019) conducted a qualitative study to investigate how students develop their attitudes toward drug use. The researchers collected data from 63 college students in 13 focus groups. A thematic approach was used, and the themes revealed that students in the college culture are expected to use drugs by peers. In other words, college students socially learn how to behave in the college environment.

However, there were several limitations in the Willis et al. (2019) study. First, because the study was conducted on college students, the findings may not necessarily apply to high school students. Second, there may be a difference between what focus group participants say and what they do. Third, dominant personalities may influence the responses of a focus group, and introverts may not effectively voice their opinions. Finally, because the study was qualitative in nature, it does not quantify relationships or make numeric predictions (Bordens & Abbott, 2008).

Fourth, Keyes et al. (2011) conducted a quantitative study to determine the relationship between society-level disapproval of marijuana and marijuana use. The researchers examined secondary data collected from 986,003 students in eighth, tenth, and twelfth grades from 1976 to 2007. Public and private schools were selected based on a multi-stage random sampling design. Data were collected from the Monitoring the Future project, which provided a nationally representative sample of adolescents. The individuals were clustered into birth cohorts to characterize the association between population-based norms and individual-level marijuana use. The researchers used odds ratio to assess the data, and the findings indicated that the use of marijuana by adolescents is influenced by fellow cohorts. In other words, social norms impact marijuana use.

However, there were several limitations in the Keyes et al. (2011) study. First, there is the possibility of systemic bias. It is possible that most of the students who participated in the study were interested in the marijuana controversy whereas those who were less interested did not participate in the study. As a result, the findings may be biased. Second, the researchers did not have information on the geographical norms for each student, and these norms may be important predictors of marijuana use. Third, students who dropped out of high school were not included in the survey estimates, which may impact the validity of the findings. Fourth, the use of a nonparametric statistic may result in some loss of efficiency for estimation of the coefficients when compared to a parametric statistic (Fitzmaurice et al., 2004; Su, 2020). Finally, because the research study was quantitative in nature, it does not describe *why* the use of marijuana by adolescents is influenced by fellow cohorts (Berg, 2007).

Fifth, Odgers et al. (2008) conducted a quantitative study to assess the association between early exposure to drugs and deviant behavior later in life. During the first stage, the researchers collected data in 1972 and 1973 from 1,037 New Zealand children during the Dunedin Multidisciplinary Health and Development Study. Follow-up assessments were conducted between 2003 and 2005 after the children turned 32 years of age. The researchers collected data on early exposure to illicit substances and conduct problems. The measure of illicit substance use during childhood was measured via self-reports, and the measure of illicit substance use during adulthood was measured via private structured interviews with the help of the fourth addition of the Diagnostic and Statistical Manual of Mental Disorders. The measure of conduct problems during childhood was measured via self, parent, and teacher reports, and the measure of conduct problems during adulthood was measured via the New Zealand Police database for both violent and non-violent crimes. The researchers then used multivariate logistic regression to calculate propensity scores for early-exposed adolescents and non-early-exposed adolescents. The researchers conducted propensity score matching, and the findings indicated that early exposure to illicit substances is positively related to substance dependency and to criminal arrest.

However, there were several limitations in the Odgers et al. (2008) study. First, study participants were not randomly selected, and propensity score matching does not test for causal relationships. Second, the participants were from New Zealand, and they may not necessarily reflect Americans. Third, the culture of drug use has changed over time, and the study did not separate cannabis from other types of drugs. Finally, because the research study was quantitative in design, it does not describe *why* the participants used illicit substances (Berg, 2007).

Finally, Pedersen and Skardhamar (2009) conducted a quantitative study to examine the relationship between marijuana use during adolescence and early adulthood and arrest later in life. Data were collected from 1992 to 2005 from a sample of 1,353 Norwegian adolescent students who participated in the Young in Norway Longitudinal Study. Data were collected from the participants when they were 13, 15, 20, and 27 years of age. The sample was stratified according to geographical area and school size. Crimes were measured by the number of charges filed against each participant for serious crimes, and the crime data were provided by Statistics Norway. Marijuana use was measured via a six-point Likert-type scale that ranged from never to more than 50 times. The participants were asked if they used marijuana in the prior 12 months. Subsequently, the researchers used multivariate analyses to assess the data, and the findings indicated that there is a relationship between early drug use and the number of arrests. However, many of the arrests were related to drug use. When all drug-related arrests were excluded from the study, the findings then indicated that there is no relationship between marijuana use and the number of arrests.

However, there were several limitations in the Pedersen and Skardhamar (2009) study. First, the number of crimes was measured by the number of arrests. Sometimes, innocent persons are arrested, and this may impact the validity of the data. Second, many offenses that are committed are not detected by the police, and, as a result, many offenders are not arrested. This may impact the validity of the data. Third, some offenders may be apprehended more easily than others, which may impact the validity of the data. Fourth, due to attrition, many serious criminal records were lost during the study, which may impact the validity of the data. Fifth, it is possible that important extraneous variables were not identified and controlled, which may impact the validity of the findings. Finally, because the research study was quantitative in nature, it does not describe *why* the participants used marijuana or committed crime (Berg, 2007).

In sum, it appears that social norms and the social environment affect the consumption of marijuana.

Siblings, friends, and peers seem to influence the behaviors of persons with whom they associate. In addition, parents recognize the importance of the social learning theory in modifying behaviors. In short, if marijuana use becomes the social norm, children may socially learn to consume marijuana as normal behavior.

III. METHODOLOGY

Political Partisanship Definition

A state was considered either Democrat or Republican based on the 2012 and 2016 U.S. Presidential elections (Presidential voting history by state, n.d.). If a state's electoral college voted for the Democrat U.S. Presidential candidate, then that state was considered a Democrat state. If a state's electoral college voted for the Republican U.S. Presidential candidate, then that state was considered a Republican state. To be considered in this study, a state had to be consistently Democrat or Republican during the years of data collection, which were 2013, 2015, and 2017.

Data Collection

The Centers for Disease Control and Prevention, which is devoted to the public's safety and health, collected data in 2013, 2015, and 2017 via the Youth Risk Behavior Surveillance System (Kann et al., 2014; Kann et al., 2016; Kann et al., 2018). A three-stage cluster sample design produced a nationally representative sample of male students in grades 9-12 who attended public and private schools across America. The standard questionnaire in 2013 included 86 questions, and the standard questionnaires in 2015 and 2017 included 89 questions.

Statistical Analysis

Because the observations for the three questionnaires used in 2013, 2015, and 2017 were from the same states, a lack of independence among the data values was expected (Su, 2020). Indeed, a prior study that used data from the same surveys over the same time period has indicated that the data values have a very large overdisperson problem (Davis, 2020). Thus, to address this parametric assumption violation, a generalized estimating equation (GEE), which is a nonparametric statistic, was used to assess the data. However, although GEE avoids the distributional assumptions of independent observations, the use of a nonparametric statistic may result in some loss of efficiency for estimation of the coefficients (Fitzmaurice et al., 2004; Su, 2020).

IV. RESULTS

Data were collected from 29 states in 2013, 23 states in 2015, and 24 states in 2017 for a total of 76 observations (see Table 1). Of all the states considered, 60.5% were Republican and 39.5% were Democrat.

The mean numbers of male high school students who have ever used marijuana for the Republican states were 267.00 (SD = 167.36), 255.23 (SD = 146.87), and 221.64 (SD = 137.59) in 2013, 2015, and 2017, respectively (see Table 2). The mean numbers of male high school students who have ever used marijuana for the Democrat states were 1216.40 (SD = 2526.56), 1169.90 (SD = 2257.15), and 940.10 (SD = 1779.20) in 2013, 2015, and 2017, respectively. The mean rates of male high school students who have ever used marijuana for the Republican states were 0.358 (SD = 0.064), 0.339 (SD = 0.049), and 0.312 (SD = 0.057) in 2013, 2015, and 2017, respectively. The mean rates of male high school students who have ever used marijuana for the Democrat states were 0.417 (SD = 0.039), 0.367 (SD = 0.037), and 0.347 (SD = 0.040) in 2013, 2015, and 2017, respectively.

Table 1. Sample Size Overview

Variable	Total number of states	Number of states (%) per political party		Number of states per year		
		Republican	Democrat	2013	2015	2017
Male high school students who have ever used marijuana	76	46 (60.5)	30 (39.5)	29	23	24

Table 2. Descriptive Statistics for the Variables of Interest

Variable	Year	Party	Number of states	Events		Events/Trials		Events/Trials			
				M	SD	M	SD	M	SD	Min	Max
Males who have ever used marijuana	2013	R	19	267.00	167.36	742.32	413.24	0.358	0.064	0.272	0.434
		D	10	1216.40	2526.56	3153.50	6754.01	0.417	0.039	0.334	0.461
	2015	R	13	255.23	146.87	739.00	376.17	0.339	0.049	0.238	0.418
		D	10	1169.90	2257.15	3481.00	6965.73	0.367	0.037	0.306	0.416
	2017	R	14	221.64	137.59	707.21	387.43	0.312	0.057	0.168	0.395
		D	10	940.10	1779.20	3012.90	6042.57	0.347	0.040	0.297	0.429
	Overall	R	46	249.87	151.01	730.70	386.85	0.339	0.060	0.168	0.434
		D	30	1108.80	2135.35	3215.80	6370.76	0.377	0.048	0.297	0.461

Note: R = Republican; D = Democrat; M = mean; SD = standard deviation; Min = minimum; Max = maximum. Events represent the number of male high school students who have ever used marijuana. Trials represent the male sample size. Events/Trials represent the rate of male high school students who have ever used marijuana.

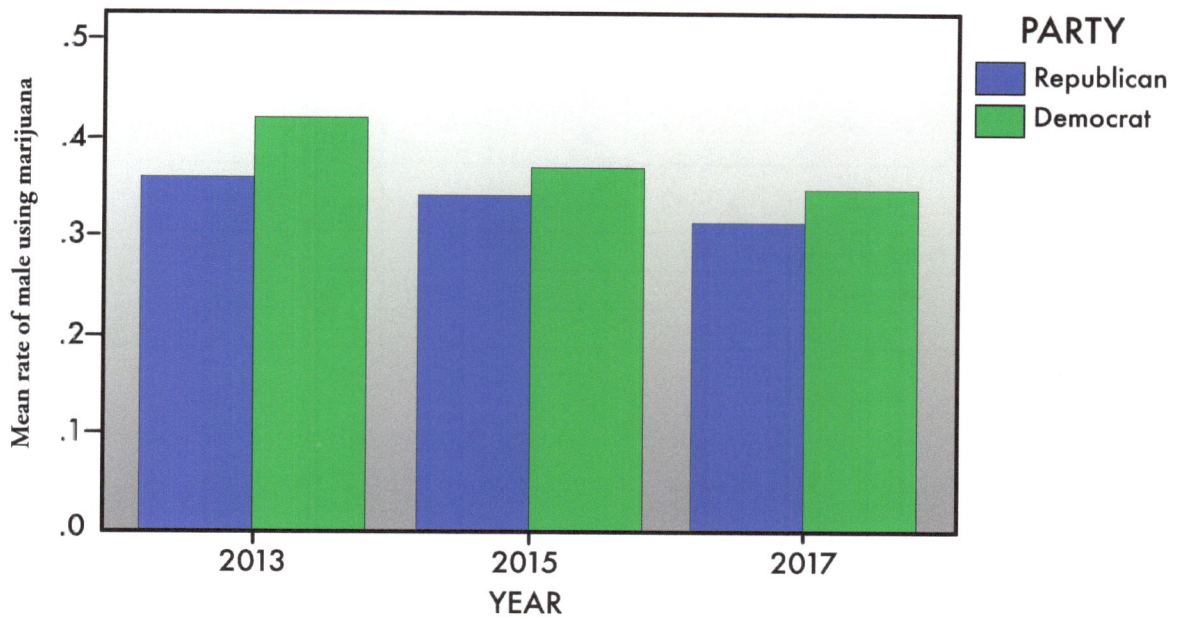

Figure 1. Bar chart of mean rates of male high school students who have ever used marijuana by year and political party.

Figure 1 shows the bar chart of mean rates of male high school students who have ever used marijuana by year and political party, which provides a direct comparison of the mean rates of male high school students who have ever used marijuana between the two political parties. Based on Figure 1, compared to Democrat states, Republican states seem to have lower mean rates of male high school students who have ever used marijuana. However, the results of the logistic regression for repeated measures indicate that there is no statistically significant relationship between male high school students who have ever used marijuana and political party ($\chi2(1) = 0.040$, $p = 0.842$, Table 3; OR = 0.987, 95% CI = [0.873, 1.117], Table 4).

Table 3. **Tests of Model Effects**			
Model	Wald $\chi2$	df	p
Male using marijuana	0.040	1	0.842

Note: Wald $\chi2$ = Wald chi-square statistic; df = degrees of freedom; p = p-value.

Table 4. Parameter Estimates and Odds Ratios

Model	Variable	B	SE	95% CI of B		OR	95% CI of OR	
				Lower	Upper		Lower	Upper
Male using marijuana	Intercept	-0.642	0.038	-0.716	-0.568			
	Political Party							
	Republican	-0.013	0.063	-0.136	0.111	0.987	0.873	1.117
	Democrat	Ref						

Note: B = parameter estimate; SE = standard error; CI = confidence interval; lower = lower bound; upper = upper bound; OR = odds ratio; ref = reference group. OR was computed as exp(B).

V. DISCUSSION

The results of the logistic regression for repeated measures indicate that there is no statistically significant relationship between male high school students who have ever used marijuana and political party. Therefore, the null hypothesis is accepted. Although the consumption of marijuana by high school students is not endorsed by either political party, the results are important because they indicate that neither political party is better than the other when it comes to creating a social learning environment that discourages marijuana use among high school students. According to the social learning theory, the social learning environment can modify a person's behavior involving the use of marijuana. Therefore, both political parties may need to consider other ways to modify the social learning environment to address the issue. To reduce the amount of male high school students who use marijuana, the proper social learning environment must be created.

Limitations

There were several limitations in this study. First, the study employed a nonparametric statistic to assess the data, which may result in some loss of efficiency for the estimation of the coefficients (Fitzmaurice et al., 2004; Su, 2020). Second, the social learning theory states that deviant and conforming behaviors are simultaneously learned and modified through the same cognitive and behavioral mechanisms (Akers & Sellers, 2009). Thus, what is actually learned in any given situation depends on the learning process within each individual. Third, because the study was quantitative in nature, it does not explain *why* male high school students used marijuana (Berg, 2007). Fourth, there is a possibility that the participants who chose to participate in the study may be different in a meaningful way from those individuals who chose not to participate, which may affect the results. Fifth, because the sample was limited to male high school students in the U.S., the findings cannot be generalized to other populations. Sixth, because the participants knew they were involved in a study, their responses may have been artificial (Bordens & Abbott, 2008). Finally, the participants may try to help the researchers by providing the answers that they believe the researchers want them to provide.

REFERENCES

Akers, R.L., & Sellers, C. (2009). *Criminological theories: Introduction, evaluation, and application* (5th ed.). New York, NY: Oxford University Press.

Armentano, P. (2012). Marijuana is not harmful, and may be beneficial, to brain health. In Merino, N. (Ed.), *Introducing issues with opposing viewpoints* (p. 18-24). Detroit, MI: Greenhaven Press.

Berg, B.L. (2007). *Qualitative research methods for the social sciences* (6th ed.). Boston, MA: Pearson Education, Inc.

Bordens, K., & Abbott, B. (2008). *Research design and methods: A process approach* (7th ed.). Boston, MA: McGraw Hill.

Burns, S. (2006). Teen marijuana use is a serious threat. In W. Aue (Ed.), *Teen Drug Abuse: Opposing viewpoints* (p. 46-50). Detroit, MI: Greenhaven Press.

Califano, J.A. (1998). Marijuana is too dangerous to legalize for medical purposes. In S.P. Thompson (Ed.), *The war on drugs: Opposing viewpoints* (p. 170-173). San Diego: Greenhaven Press.

Cobb-Clark, D.A., Kassenboehmer, S.C., Le, T., McVicar, D., & Zhang, R. (2015). 'High'-school: The relationship between early marijuana use and educational outcomes. *Economic Record, 91*(293), 247-266.

Davis, W.L. (2020). Is There a Difference Between Democrat and Republican States in the Number of Female Students Who Experienced Cyberbullying? *Lincoln Memorial Journal of Social Sciences, 1*(1), Article 1.

Eisenberg, N., Jones, T.M., Kosterman, R., Bailey, J.A., Lee, J.O., & Haggerty, K.P. (2019). Parenting practices in the context of legal marijuana: Voices from Seattle parents. *Journal of Child and Family Studies, 28,* 587-598. doi: 10.1007/s10826-018-1288-9

Fanning, K. (2011). Marijuana is very bad for teens. In D.E. Nelson (Ed.), *Teen Drug Abuse: Opposing viewpoints* (p. 52-56). Detroit, MI: Greenhaven Press.

Fitzmaurice, G. M., Laird, N. M., & Ware, J. H. (2004). *Applied longitudinal analysis.* Hoboken, NJ: John Wiley & Sons.

Foundation for a Drug-Free World (2020). *The truth about marijuana.* https://www.drugfreeworld.org/drugfacts/marijuana/international-statistics.html

Kann, L., Kinchen, S., Shanklin, S.L., Flint, K.H., Hawkins, J., Harris, W.A., . . . Zaza, S. (2014). Youth risk behavior surveillance—United States, 2013. *Morbidity and Mortality Weekly Report: Surveillance Summaries, 63*(4), 1-172. https://www.cdc.gov/mmwr/pdf/ss/ss6304.pdf

Kann, L., McManus, T., Harris, W.A., Shanklin, S.L., Flint, K.H., Hawkins, . . . Zaza, S. (2015). Youth risk behavior surveillance—United States, 2015. *Morbidity and Mortality Weekly Report: Surveillance Summaries, 65*(6), 1-180. https://www.cdc.gov/healthyyouth/data/yrbs/pdf/2015/ss6506_updated.pdf

Kann, L., McManus, T., Harris, W.A., Shanklin, S.L., Flint, K.H., Hawkins, J., Queen, B., . . . Ethier, K.A. (2018). Youth risk behavior surveillance—United States, 2017. *Morbidity and Mortality Weekly Report: Surveillance Summaries, 67*(8), 1-479. https://www.cdc.gov/healthyyouth/data/yrbs/pdf/2017/ss6708.pdf

Keyes, K.M., Schulenberg, J.E., O'Malley, P.M., Johnston, L.D., Bachman, J.G., Li, G., & Hasin, D. (2011). The social norms of birth cohorts and adolescent marijuana use in the United States, 1976-2007. *Addiction, 106*, 1790-1800. doi: 10.1111/j.1360-0443.2011.03485.x

Keyhani, S., Steigerwald, S., Ishida, J., Vali, M., Cerdá, M., Hasin, D., Dollinger, C., Yoo, S.R. Cohen, B.E. (2018). Risks and Benefits of Marijuana Use: A National Survey of U.S. Adults. *Annals of Internal Medicine, 169* (5), 282-290.

Moline, M. (1998). Courts should emphasize rehabilitation over punishment. In S.P. Thompson (Ed.), *The war on drugs: Opposing viewpoints* (p. 199-203). San Diego, CA: Greenhaven Press.

Odgers, C.L., Caspi, A., Nagin, D.S., Piquero, A.R., Slutske, W.S., Milne, B.J., Dickson, N., Poulton, R. & Moffitt, T.E. (2008). Is it important to prevent early exposure to drugs and alcohol among adolescents? *Association for Psychological Science, 19*(10), 1037-1044.

Pedersen, W., & Skardhamar, T. (2009). Cannabis and crime: Findings from a longitudinal study. *Addiction, 105*(1), 109-118. doi: 10.1111/j.1360-0443.2009.02719.x

Porter, M. (2012). Marijuana is harmful to physical and mental health. In Merino, N. (Ed.), *Introducing issues with opposing viewpoints* (p. 12-17). Detroit, MI: Greenhaven Press.

Presidential voting history by state (n.d.). https://ballotpedia.org/Presidential_voting_ history_by_state

Snyder, R.L. (2016). *The sport of politics simplified: Democrats versus Republicans, the 2016 spectator's guide.* North Charleston, SC: Createspace.

Stimson, C.D. (2012). Marijuana is much more harmful than alcohol. In Merino, N. (Ed.), *Introducing issues with opposing viewpoints* (p. 25-30). Detroit, MI: Greenhaven Press.

Su, Y. (2020). *Dr. Su Statistics.* https://sites.google.com/site/drsustat/

Verweij, K.J.H., Zietsch, B.P., Lynskey, M.T., Medland, S.E., Neale, M.C., Martin, N.G., Boomsma, D.I., & Vink, J.M. (2010). Genetic and environmental influences on cannabis use initiation and problematic use: a meta-analysis of twin studies. *Addiction, 105*(3), 417-430.

Walters, J.P. (2005). Marijuana is harmful. T.L. Roleff (Ed.), Drug Abuse: *Opposing viewpoints* (p. 18-22). Detroit, MI: Greenhaven Press.

Willis, E., Adams, R., & Keene, J. (2019). If everyone is doing it, it must be safe: College students' development of attitudes toward poly-substance use. *Substance Use & Misuse, 54*(11), 1886-1893.

Political Partisanship and Female High School Students Who Physically Fight on Campus

Chance Honeycutt, Lincoln Memorial University (TN)
&
Wayne L. Davis, Ph.D., Columbia College (SC)

Abstract

Democrats and Republicans have different platforms on how to modify the social learning environment. According to the social learning theory, people learn to be aggressive through their life experiences. These experiences include personally observing the behaviors of others and modeling them. Personal behaviors are a product of learning the norms, values, and behaviors of society. Indeed, learning is a by-product of the interaction with others and is influenced by perceptions of the legal code. Because people experience culture conflict when they are exposed to different and opposing attitudes of acceptable behaviors, and because Democrats and Republicans have different attitudes toward marijuana, gun control, and religion, it is unclear if the different social learning environments created by the two different political parties will influence high school violence. Therefore, the purpose of this study was to determine if there is a difference between political partisanship and the percentage of female high school students who physically fight on campus in each jurisdiction. This study examined electronic second-hand data collected in 2013, 2015, and 2017 by the Centers for Disease Control and Prevention. The results of the logistic regression for repeated measures indicate that there is a statistically significant relationship between female high school students who physically fight on campus and political party. Females were 35.6% less likely to physically fight on campus in Republican states than in Democrat states.

I. INTRODUCTION

Democrats and Republicans have different platforms on how to modify the social learning environment. First, many Democrats support legalizing recreational marijuana because it is commonly used and socially acceptable (Snyder, 2016). Republicans, on the other hand, oppose legalizing recreational marijuana because they believe it is a threat to the health and safety of the public. Second, Democrats support gun-control laws because they believe that the behavior of criminals can be modified in a good way through the elimination of guns. Republicans, on the other hand, oppose gun-control laws because they believe that the behavior of criminals will be modified in a bad way. In other words, if the law-abiding residents give up their guns, then the social environment will be optimistic for criminal behaviors. Third, Democrats and Republicans have different philosophies on religion (DeMint, 2020; Snyder, 2016). Democrats believe that God and religion should be removed from the government and the power of the government is the moral authority. Republicans, on the other hand, believe God and religion are the foundations of America and God's word is the guiding moral authority on how Americans should behave. In short, Democrats and Republicans create two different social learning environments via the passage of laws. Each party will support laws to create the environment that furthers its agenda.

This study will investigate whether there is a difference between political party and the amount of female high school student violence. According to the social learning theory, people learn to be aggressive through their life experiences (Siegel, 2018). These experiences include personally observing the behaviors of others and modeling them. Personal behaviors are a product of learning the norms, values, and behaviors of society. Indeed, learning is a by-product of the interaction with others and is influenced by perceptions of the legal code. Because people experience culture conflict when they are exposed to different and opposing attitudes of acceptable behaviors, and because Democrats and Republicans have different attitudes toward marijuana, gun control, and religion, it is unclear if the different social learning environments created by the two different political parties will influence high school violence.

Because public safety is a desirable social goal, it is important to investigate whether there is a difference between the Democrat-created social environment and the Republican-created social environment. Therefore, the purpose of this study was to determine if there is a difference between political partisanship and the percentage of female high school students who fight on campus in each jurisdiction. The research question and the null hypothesis are listed below.

Research Question: Is there a difference between Democrat and Republican states in the percentage of female high school students who physically fight on school property?

Null Hypothesis: There is no difference between Democrat and Republican states in the percentage of female high school students who physically fight on school property.

II. LITERATURE REVIEW

Three factors will be reviewed involving the social learning environment: marijuana use, gun-control policies, and religion. These factors are important because there are clear differences between the two political parties on these topics (DeMint, 2020; Snyder, 2016). The Democrats are liberal on marijuana use, strict on gun-control policies, and believe the government should be free from religion. The Republicans, on the other hand, are strict on marijuana use, oppose strict gun-control policies, and believe religion should play a visible role in the government.

Marijuana Use

For a study that supports the Democrats, Morris et al. (2014) conducted a longitudinal study to assess the relationship between medical marijuana legalization and the number of Part I Uniform Crime Reporting offenses. Data for Part 1 crimes for each state were collected from 1990 to 2006. The researchers used fixed-effects ordinary least squares regression models to assess the data, and the findings indicated that there is no relationship between medical marijuana laws and officially reported Part 1 crimes.

However, there were several limitations in the Morris et al. (2014) study. First, the Uniform Crime Reporting data used in the study did not include juvenile crimes. Second, the Uniform Crime Reporting data did not consider crimes not reported to the police. Thus, the crime data used in the study were less than optimal, which may affect the validity of the study. Third, there is the possibility that some extraneous variables were not considered, which may affect the nature of the relationship between the variables Fourth, fixed-effect models are vulnerable to time-varying factors, which may differ between states with and without medical marijuana laws. Finally, because the study was quantitative in nature, it does not determine the reasons *why* variables are or are not related.

For a study that supports the Republicans, Shorey et al. (2016) conducted a study to determine if marijuana use is related to dating violence. One-hundred seventy-three female undergraduate students from a public university in the Southeastern United States agreed to participate in a 90-day daily diary study. Each participant was at least 18 years of age, she was in a current relationship with a partner who was at least 18 years of age, she saw her dating partner at least twice per week, and she consumed alcohol in the previous month. In addition, each participant recorded whether she used marijuana immediately before she was victimization by her partner. Each participant recorded information in her 90-day daily diary about her contact with her dating partner, her dating violence victimization, her alcohol use, her marijuana use, and her partner's substance use. The researchers used multilevel modeling to examine the odds of being victimized, and the findings indicated that marijuana increases the odds of being psychologically and sexually victimized.

However, there were several limitations in the Shorey et al. (2016) study. First, because the sample was primarily Caucasian females, the findings may not necessarily be generalized to other populations. Second, data were only collected from the participants and not from their dating partners. It may be important to examine the substance use of the partners when assessing the odds of dating violence. Third, the participants were asked to indicate if they used marijuana immediately before the victimization, but the length of time was not specified. Fourth, the researchers did not allow the participants to indicate if they were dating multiple partners or if they were victimized more than once per day. Finally, the researchers did not have information on females who qualified for the study but decided not to participate. Individuals who did not participate may have been different in a systematic way from the individuals who chose to participate.

Gun-Control Policies

For a study that supports the Democrats, Kaufman et al. (2018) have conducted a cross-sectional study to determine if there is a relationship between the distance that counties are located from states with lenient gun-control policies and the number of gun-related deaths. The researchers examined the U.S. Centers for Disease Control and Prevention's gun-related death rates for 3,108 counties in the 48 contiguous states in America from 2010 to 2014. The researchers used multilevel Bayesian spatial Poisson models to generate incident rate ratios, and the findings indicated that strong firearm laws are inversely related to the number of firearm homicides and firearm suicides, regardless of the firearm laws in adjacent states. In addition, there is an inverse relationship between strong gun-control policies in adjacent states and the number of gun-related deaths in states with weak gun-control laws.

However, there were several limitations in the Kaufman et al. (2018) study. First, because the available data only contained a few states with very strict gun-control laws, the researchers were unable to effectively detect an effect of the strictest gun-control laws. Second, evidence from the FBI indicated that guns discovered at crime scenes often migrated there from distant states. Third, the laws were grouped together in a way that masked the effect of any particular law. Fourth, it is unclear if unmeasured variables may have impacted the adoption of firearm laws and death rates. Finally, the study examined correlational relationships and not causal relationships.

For a study that supports the Republicans, Moorhouse and Wanner (2006) conducted a study to determine if the number of gun-control measures is negatively related to the number of gun-related crimes in the state. Data were collected from all 50 states and from the District of Columbia for laws that were in place in 1998. The laws were grouped into six categories: 1) Registration laws, 2) Safety training requirements, 3) Regulation of firearm sales, 4) Safety storage, 5) Ownership licensing, and 6) the Presence of more restrictive city or county ordinances. The researchers employed regression analysis to assess the data, and the findings indicated that there is no significant relationship between the number of gun-control measures and the number of gun-related crimes in the state. In addition, the findings indicated that there is no relationship between neighboring states having lax gun-control laws and the number of crimes in the state with gun-control laws.

However, there were several limitations in the Moorhouse and Wanner (2006) study. First, there are aggregation problems when state data are used, which could mask relationships in the data. Second, many of the gun-control laws since 1998 have changed, which make the findings less than applicable in today's culture. Finally, because the study was quantitative in nature, it investigated *how* variables were related, but it did not investigate *why* existing laws were not effective.

Religion

For a study that supports the Democrats, Yilmaz et al. (2016) conducted a study to investigate the causal effect of religious beliefs and analytic thinking on prejudice toward out-groups. The sample was comprised of 127 Muslim undergraduate students from Boğaziçi University in Turkey. The sample was comprised of 80 females, 47 males, and one individual who did not identify a specific sex. Data were collected via online surveys. The researchers conducted a between-subjects ANOVA and a Tukey Honestly Significance Difference post hoc test to assess the differences between religious individuals, analytical individuals, and neutral individuals. The findings indicated that the negative attitudes of the analytical individuals are not significantly different from the negative attitudes of the neutral individuals. However, the findings also indicated that 1) persons who scored high or moderately high in religiosity are more prejudice than individuals who scored low in religiosity, and 2) religious individuals are more prejudice than the analytical or neutral individuals.

However, there were several limitations in the Yilmaz et al. (2016) study. First, the study was conducted in Turkey, which has a different social learning environment than the U.S. Second, the study was conducted on college students, and the findings may not necessarily apply to high school students. Third, the researchers had to change some of the language on the Intuitive Religious Belief Scale because some of the items were unclear when translated to Turkish. Changing the wording of the questions may negatively affect the validity of the data. Finally, the study assessed *how* variables were numerically related but not *why* they were related.

For a study that supports the Republicans, Pearce et al. (2003) conducted a one-year longitudinal study to assess whether religiosity and parent involvement were related to student conduct problems. Religiosity was measured by one's a) frequency of attending religious services, b) frequency of engaging in informal religious practices, c) beliefs about God, and d) personal evaluation of being religious. The researchers collected data from 1,703 high-risk urban students in Northeastern United States who were in 6th to 8th grade. The sample was comprised of about 53% females and 61% African Americans. The researchers applied hierarchical multiple regression to analyze the data, and the findings indicated that religiosity and parent involvement are related to fewer conduct problems. In addition, the relationship between exposure to violence and misconduct is moderated by religiosity, which diminishes the negative effects of exposure to violence.

However, there were several limitations in the Pearce et al. (2003) study. First, because the data were collected using a self-administered survey, and because the students were being asked about violence and misconduct, there is the possibility that they were less than truthful in their responses. Second, because the participants were in 6th to 8th grade, the findings may not necessarily apply to high school students. Third, because the participants resided in the Northeastern United States, the findings may not necessarily apply to populations in other geographical locations. Fourth, because the study used a cross-sectional survey design, causal relationships cannot be determined. Finally, because the study was quantitative in nature, it does explain the motive behind the participants' behaviors.

In sum, as explained by the social learning theory, individuals may learn either pro-social or anti-social behaviors in a specific social learning environment (Siegel, 2018). Hence, it is difficult to say how the social learning environment, as created by the political parties, may impact the behaviors of high school students. Because public safety is an important social goal, it is important to know if there is a difference between Democrat and Republican jurisdictions and violent behaviors among high school students.

III. METHODOLOGY

Political Partisanship Definition

A state was considered either Democrat or Republican based on the U.S. Presidential elections for 2012 and 2016 ("Presidential Voting History by State," n.d.). If a state's electoral college voted for the Democrat U.S. Presidential candidate, then that state was considered a Democrat state. If a state's electoral college voted for the Republican U.S. Presidential candidate, then that state was considered a Republican state. To be considered in this study, a state had to be consistently Democrat or Republican during the years of data collection, which were 2013, 2015, and 2017.

Sample

The Centers for Disease Control and Prevention collected data via the Youth Risk Behavior Surveillance System in 2013, 2015, and 2017 (Kann et al., 2014; Kann et al., 2016; Kann et al., 2018). Data were collected using a three-stage cluster sample design, which produced a nationally representative sample of U.S. female high school students in grades 9–12 who attended public and private schools. The standard questionnaire in 2013 included 86 questions, and the standard questionnaires in 2015 and 2017 included 89 questions.

Statistical Analysis

Because data were collected from the same states over three collection periods, data may have been collected from the same participants for more than one survey (Kann et al., 2014; Kann et al., 2016; Kann et al., 2018). For example, students surveyed in 9th grade may have also been surveyed in 11th grade. Students surveyed in 10th grade may have also been surveyed in 12th grade. In other words, the data values were not expected to be independent. This was confirmed in a prior study that used the same data source, which indicated a very large overdisperson problem (Davis, 2020). Thus, to address this parametric statistic assumption violation, a generalized estimating equation (GEE), which is a nonparametric statistic, was used to assess the data. However, the use of a nonparametric statistic may result in some loss of efficiency for the estimation of the coefficients (Fitzmaurice et al., 2004; Su, 2020).

IV. RESULTS

Data were collected from 28 states in 2013, 26 states in 2015, and 25 states in 2017 for a total of 79 observations (see Table 1). Of all the states considered, 62% were Republican and 38% were Democrat. The mean numbers of females who physically fought at school for the Republican states were 39.58 (SD = 17.98), 38.07 (SD = 29.68), and 28.13 (SD = 14.16) in 2013, 2015, and 2017, respectively (see Table 2). The mean numbers of females who physically fought at school for the Democrat states were 301.00 (SD = 721.45), 245.18 (SD = 553.62), and 222.00 (SD = 512.39) in 2013, 2015, and 2017, respectively. The mean rates of females who physically fought at school for the Republican states were 0.056 (SD = 0.019), 0.046 (SD = 0.013), and 0.043 (SD = 0.017) in 2013, 2015, and 2017, respectively. The mean rates of females who physically fought at school for the Democrat states were 0.054 (SD = 0.025), 0.051 (SD = 0.017), and 0.051 (SD = 0.022) in 2013, 2015, and 2017, respectively.

Table 1. Sample Size Overview						
		Number of states (%) per political party		Number of states per year		
Variable	Total number of observations	Republican	Democrat	2013	2015	2017
Females who physically fought	79	49 (62.0)	38 (38.0)	28	26	25

Variable	Year	Party	Number of states	Events		Trials		Events/Trials			
				M	SD	M	SD	M	SD	Min	Max
Females who physically fought	2013	R	19	39.58	17.98	733.47	377.33	0.056	0.019	0.035	0.109
		D	9	301.00	721.45	3529.44	6881.59	0.054	0.025	0.026	0.102
	2015	R	15	38.07	29.68	779.33	399.75	0.046	0.013	0.031	0.077
		D	11	245.18	553.62	3704.36	6361.53	0.051	0.017	0.023	0.085
	2017	R	15	28.13	14.16	682.73	348.58	0.043	0.017	0.021	0.095
		D	10	222.00	512.39	3115.60	5724.42	0.051	0.022	0.019	0.087
	Overall	R	49	35.61	21.50	731.98	370.00	0.049	0.018	0.021	0.109
		D	30	254.20	576.04	3455.63	6103.55	0.052	0.021	0.019	0.102

Note: R = Republican; D = Democrat; M = mean; SD = standard deviation; Min = minimum; Max = maximum. Events represent the number of females who physically fought at school. Trials represent the female sample size. Events/Trials represent the rate of females who physically fought at school.

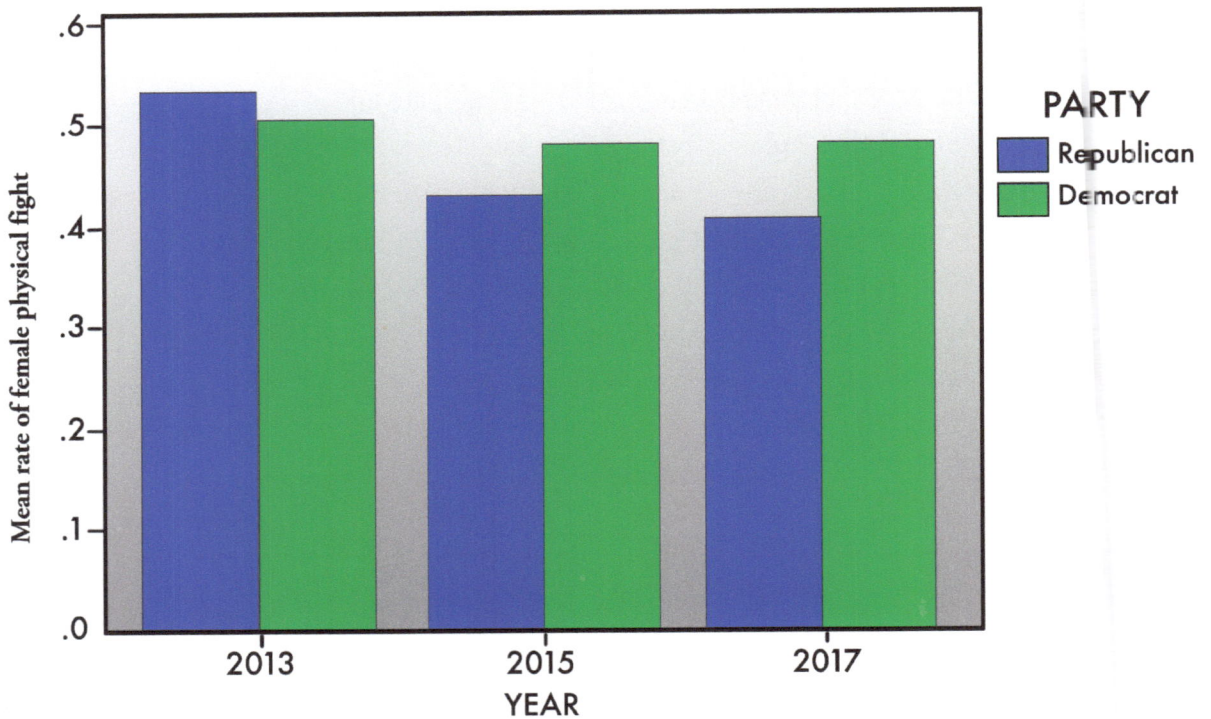

Figure 1. Bar chart of mean rates of female high school students who physically fought on campus by year and political party.

Figure 1 shows the bar chart of mean rates of females who physically fought by year and political party, which provides a direct comparison of the mean rates of females who physically fought at school between the two political parties. Compared to the mean rates in the Democrat states, except for 2013, the mean rates of females who physically fought at school seem to be lower in the Republican states. Indeed, the results of the logistic regression for repeated measures indicate that there is a statistically significant relationship between females who physically fight at school and political party ($\chi2(1) = 5.591$, $p = 0.018$, Table 3). In particular, females were 35.6% less likely to physically fight at schools in Republican states than in Democrat states (OR = 0.644, 95% CI = [0.447, 0.927], Table 4).

Table 3. **Tests of Model Effects**			
Model	Wald $\chi2$	df	p
Females who physically fight on campus	5.591	1	0.018

Note: Wald $\chi2$ = Wald chi-square statistic; df = degrees of freedom; p = p-value.

Table 4. **Parameter Estimates and Odds Ratios**								
Model	Variable	B	SE	95% CI of B		OR	95% CI of OR	
				Lower	Upper		Lower	Upper
Females who physically fight on campus	Intercept	-2.533	.1757	-2.878	-2.189			
	Political Party							
	Republican	-0.440	0.186	-0.805	-0.075	0.644	0.447	0.927
	Democrat	Ref						

Note: B = parameter estimate; SE = standard error; CI = confidence interval; lower = lower bound; upper = upper bound; OR = odds ratio; ref = reference group. OR was computed as exp(B).

V. DISCUSSION

The results of the logistic regression for repeated measures indicate that there is a statistically significant relationship between female high school students who physically fight on campus and political party. Females were 35.6% less likely to physically fight on campus in Republican states than in Democrat states. Therefore, the null hypothesis is rejected. The results of this study are important because they indicate that the social learning environment created by the Republicans seem to decrease the number of fights on campus for female high school students. In short, the problem of fighting on campus may be addressed through appropriate laws that create the proper social learning environment.

Limitations

There were several limitations in this study. First, not all states and large urban school districts included all of the standard questions on their Youth Risk Behavior Surveillance System questionnaires (Kann et al, 2016). Second, the history factor may have affected the study's internal validity. In other words, specific events, other than the treatment, may have occurred between multiple observations, which may have affected the results (Bordens & Abbott, 2008). Third, the social learning theory fails to adequately consider a) how other people help an individual construct the social world, b) how an individual acquires shared representations of social and interpersonal phenomena, and c) how some developmental routes are encouraged and some are inhibited as a result of particular social arrangements (Durkin, 1995). Fourth, because the sample was limited to female high school students in the U.S., the findings cannot necessarily be generalized to individuals who do not match the sample's characteristics. Fifth, because the study was quantitative in nature, it does not explain *why* female high school students physically fight on campus (Berg, 2007). Finally, the participants may have provided responses that reflect the way that they want to see themselves.

REFERENCES

Berg, B.L. (2007). *Qualitative research methods for the social sciences* (6th ed.). Boston, MA: Pearson Education, Inc.

Bordens, K., & Abbott, B. (2008). *Research design and methods: A process approach* (7th ed.). Boston, MA: McGraw Hill.

Davis, W.L. (2020). Is There a Difference Between Democrat and Republican States in the Number of Female Students Who Experienced Cyberbullying? *Lincoln Memorial Journal of Social Sciences, 1*(1), Article 1.

DeMint, J. (2020). *They're lying to you! 10 lies that shape your truth.* Washington, DC: Conservative Partner Institute.

Durkin, K. (1995). *Developmental social psychology: From infancy to old age.* Boston, MA: Blackwell Publishing Company.

Fitzmaurice, G. M., Laird, N. M., & Ware, J. H. (2004). *Applied longitudinal analysis.* Hoboken, NJ: John Wiley & Sons.

Kann, L., Kinchen, S., Shanklin, S.L., Flint, K.H., Hawkins, J., Harris, W.A., . . . Zaza, S. (2014). Youth risk behavior surveillance—United States, 2013. *Morbidity and Mortality Weekly Report: Surveillance Summaries, 63*(4), 1-172. https://www.cdc.gov/mmwr/pdf/ss/ss6304.pdf

Kann, L., McManus, T., Harris, W.A., Shanklin, S.L., Flint, K.H., Hawkins, . . . Zaza, S. (2016). Youth risk behavior surveillance—United States, 2015. *Morbidity and Mortality Weekly Report: Surveillance Summaries, 65*(6), 1-180. https://www.cdc.gov/healthyyouth/data/yrbs/pdf/2015/ss6506_updated.pdf

Kann, L., McManus, T., Harris, W.A., Shanklin, S.L., Flint, K.H., Hawkins, J., Queen, B., . . . Ethier, K.A. (2018). Youth risk behavior surveillance—United States, 2017. *Morbidity and Mortality Weekly Report: Surveillance Summaries, 67*(8), 1-479. https://www.cdc.gov/healthyyouth/data/yrbs/pdf/2017/ss6708.pdf

Kaufman, E.J., Morrison, C.N., Branas, C.C., & Wiebe, D.J. (2018). State firearm laws and interstate firearm deaths from homicide and suicide in the United States: A cross-sectional analysis of data by county. *JAMA Internal Medicine, 178*(5), 692-700. doi: 10.1001/jamainternmed.2018.0190

Moorhouse, J.C., & Wanner, B. (2006). Does gun control reduce crime or does crime increase gun control? *Cato Journal, 26*(1), 103-124.

Morris, R.G., TenEyck, M., Barnes, J.C., & Kovandzic, T.V. (2014). The effect of medical marijuana laws on crime: Evidence from state panel data, 1990-2006. *PLoS ONE, 9*(3), 1-7.

Pearce, M.J., Jones, S.M., Schwab-Stone, M.E., & Ruchkin, V. (2003). The protective effects of religiousness and parent involvement on the development of conduct problems among youth exposed to violence. *Child Development, 74*(6), 1682-1696.

Presidential voting history by state (n.d.). https://ballotpedia.org/Presidential_voting_history_by_state

Shorey, R.C., Moore, T.M., McNulty, J.K., & Stuart, G.L. (2016). Do Alcohol and Marijuana Increase the Risk for Female Dating Violence Victimization? A Prospective Daily Diary Investigation. *Psychology of Violence, 6*(4), 509-518. doi: 10.1037/a0039943

Siegel, L.J. (2018). *Criminology: Theories, patterns, and typologies* (13th ed.). Boston, MA: Cengage.

Snyder, R.L. (2016). *The sport of politics simplified: Democrats versus Republicans, the 2016 spectator's guide.* North Charleston, SC: Createspace.

Su, Y. (2020). *Dr. Su Statistics.* https://sites.google.com/site/drsustat/

Yilmaz, O., Karadoller, D.Z., & Sofuoglu, G. (2016). Analytic thinking, religion, and prejudice: An experimental test of the dual-process model of mind. *The International Journal for the Psychology of Religion, 26*(4), 360-369. doi: 10.1080/10508619.2016.1151117

Political Partisanship and Male High School Students Who Physically Fight on Campus

Anthony Brown, Lincoln Memorial University (TN)
&
Wayne Davis, Ph.D., Columbia College (SC)

Abstract

School violence is a common occurrence in American high schools. Victims of school violence are more likely than others to become depressed, skip school, and commit suicide. In addition, intimidation, threats, sexual harassment, prejudice, gossip, and ridicule are serious threats to successful education Overall, about 33% of students are bullied at school by other students, and bullying leads to fights. Because Democrats and Republicans support two different types of social learning environments that will modify the behaviors of residents within their respective jurisdictions, and because public safety is an important social issue, it is important to know if there is a difference between Democrat and Republican jurisdictions and aggressive behaviors of high school students. Therefore the purpose of this study was to determine if there is a difference between Democrat and Republican states in the percentage of male high school students who physically fight on campus. This study examined electronic second-hand data collected in 2013, 2015, and 2017 by the Centers for Disease Control and Prevention. Data were collected via the Youth Risk Behavior Surveillance System (YRBSS) using a three-stage cluster sample design, which produced a nationally representative sample of students in grades 9-12 who attended public and private schools. The results of the logistic regression for repeated measures indicate that there is no statistically significant relationship between male high school students who physically fight on campus and political party.

I. INTRODUCTION

School Violence

School violence is a common occurrence in American high schools (Barbour, 2006). Victims of school violence are more likely than others to become depressed, skip school, and commit suicide. In addition, intimidation, threats, sexual harassment, prejudice, gossip, and ridicule are serious threats to successful education. Overall, about 33% of students are bullied at school by other students, and bullying leads to fights (Chew, 2016). To make schools safer, zero-tolerance policies have been implemented (Mattiuzzi, 2011). However, zero-tolerance policies have shown to be ineffective. Because force alone cannot be used to eliminate the problem, the behavior of students needs to be modified through the social learning environment.

Social Learning Theory

According to the social learning theory, pro-social and anti-social behaviors are learned through the same cognitive and behavioral mechanisms, learning is an on-going process, and people learn through experience and observation (Akers & Sellers, 2009). Personal behaviors are reinforced according to the intensity, frequency, importance, and duration of the social learning experiences. Because Democrats and Republicans create different social learning environments, what is learned in the Democrat-controlled environment may be different than what is learned in the Republican-controlled environment. Because school violence is a public health issue, it is important to know if there is a difference in the amount of high school violence in the two different social learning environments.

Social Learning Environments

Democrats and Republicans support laws and policies that create unique social learning environments. For example, the Democrats believe that the government should promote freedom from religion and that marijuana use is acceptable in today's culture (Snyder, 2016). Republicans, on the other hand, believe that the government should promote freedom of religion and that marijuana use is unacceptable because it is harmful and leads to crime. Because the political parties influence laws, Democrats and Republicans create two different types of social learning environments that will influence the behaviors of high school students.

Religiosity & Marijuana Use

Religiosity and the use of marijuana have been linked to personal behaviors, such as aggression and crime (Blogowska et al., 2013; Dunlap & Johnson, 1996). Because religion and marijuana use are political issues, and because the government runs society, it is important to know if one social learning environment is worse than the other in terms of violence and crime. Because the behaviors of children will be molded by the government-created environment, this study will investigate if there is a difference between political partisanship and the percentage of male high school students who physically fight on campus. The research question and the null hypothesis are listed below.

Research Question: Is there a difference between Democrat and Republican states in the percentage of male high school students who physically fight on campus?

Null Hypothesis: There is no difference between Democrat and Republican states in the percentage of male high school students who physically fight on campus.

II. LITERATURE REVIEW

According to Akers' social learning theory, behaviors are reinforced over time according to the intensity, duration, importance, and frequency of social learning experiences (Akers & Sellers, 2009). However, pro-social and anti-social behaviors are simultaneously learned and modified through the same cognitive and behavioral mechanisms. Hence, it is unclear exactly what behaviors individuals will learn in a specific social learning environment. The review of the literature will focus on religiosity, marijuana use, and the learning of behaviors, which are important because the Democrats and Republicans support two different types of social learning environments that will modify the behaviors of residents within their respective jurisdictions.

Religiosity

First, Blogowska et al. (2013) conducted a quantitative study to assess the relationship between religiosity and aggressive behaviors. The sample consisted of 130 undergraduate college students in Belgium. One hundred fifteen of the participants were female, 88 identified themselves as believers in God, and 42 identified themselves as nonbelievers. Each participant read a paper about technological progress (the control condition) and then read a paper about the social progress in the acceptance of gay rights (the experimental condition). Each participant was then led to believe that the author of each paper was participating in another study dedicated to taste preferences. Each participant was to provide hot sauce to the perceived authors of the papers. The researchers measured aggressive behaviors by measuring the amount of hot sauce the participants provided to the perceived authors (more hot sauce meant more aggression). Subsequently, the researchers used a moderated regression analysis to assess the data. As a result, the findings indicated that religiosity was positively related to aggressive behaviors when the participants were dealing with moral out-group members but not when dealing with moral in-group members. The findings for aggression were validated via the self-reported Buss-Perry Aggression Questionnaire, and the findings for explicit anti-gay prejudice were validated via the European Social Survey.

However, there were several limitations in the Blogowska et al. (2013) study. First, hot sauce allocation may not be the best way to measure aggression, and the technique does not measure covert aggression. Second, it is unclear if the hot sauce was given to the perceived authors because they were believed to be gay or because they were believed to be advocates of gay rights. Third, although regression analysis is effective for determining linear relationships, it is not good for determining nonlinear relationships. Fourth, because the participants resided in Belgium, the findings may not necessarily apply to American students. Finally, quantitative studies do not provide an in-depth understanding of the meanings that the participants associated with their lived experiences (Berg, 2007).

Second, Davis (2018) conducted a study to assess the relationship between religiosity and verbal aggression. The sample was comprised of 255 African American females who had graduated from high school and who were from 21 to 40 years of age. Data for aggression were collected via the Aggression Questionnaire, and data for religiosity were collected via the Religious Emphasis Scale. Data on personal, family, and social risk factors were also collected and assessed. The researcher used multiple regression to assess the data, and the findings indicated that childhood religiosity was positively related to verbal aggression.

However, there were several limitations in Davis (2018) study. First, the sample was comprised of African American female adults, who may not necessarily reflect the participants in the current study (i.e., male high school students). Second, because the sample was convenient, purposive, and non-random, there is a possibility that the individuals who chose to participate in the study were different in a meaningful way from the individuals who chose not to participate. Third, the study had a correlational design and cannot determine causal relationships. Finally, because the study had a quantitative design, it cannot provide the meanings and motivations behind the participants' behaviors.

Third, Baier and Wright (2001) conducted a meta-analysis to assess the relationship between religiosity and crime. The researchers identified 60 studies on religiosity that were produced from 1969 to 1998. Behavioral measures included items such as attending church, watching religious television shows, listening to religious radio stations, praying, and having family discussions. Attitudinal measures included strength of religious beliefs and importance of religion. The researchers used Pearson's r to assess the data, and the findings indicated that religiosity was inversely related to criminal behaviors.

However, there were several limitations in the Baier and Wright (2001) study. First, journals often fail to publish studies that report non-significant results. Consequently, studies that have been performed, which have produced non-significant findings, may not have been available for the researchers to examine. Second, because the meta-analysis study did not allow for the manipulation of the independent variables, causal relationships cannot be determined. Finally, because the study had a quantitative design, it failed to explain *why* people did or did not commit crimes.

Finally, Jang and Johnson (2001) conducted a five-year longitudinal study to determine whether personal commitments to religiosity and religious networks buffer children against anti-social behaviors. The researchers used self-reported data collected by the National Youth Survey from 1,087 children who were 11 to 17 years of age. The sample was representative of children living in the continental U.S. The researchers applied hierarchical linear models to analyze the data, and the findings indicated that there was an inverse relationship between religiosity and anti-social behaviors and that the effect became stronger as the children matured.

However, there were several limitations in the Jang and Johnson (2001) study. First, religiosity was measured solely by church attendance. This could be problematic because some children may feel that they are religious even though they may not have attended church. Second, because the data were collected using self-reports, some children may have been less than truthful in disclosing their deviant behaviors, especially in highly religious environments. Finally, because the study had a quantitative design, it does not explain the reasons *why* the participants engaged in deviant behaviors (Berg, 2007).

Drug Environment

First, Dunlap and Johnson (1996) conducted an in-depth ethnographic case study to assess whether children who were exposed to a drug environment had learned to be aggressive. The researchers developed relationships with crack sellers and their families through the Natural History of Crack Distribution/Abuse project, which was funded by the National Institute for Drug Abuse. The researchers recruited the Jones and Smith family and collected data through personal interviews, observations, and field notes for three years. The researchers recorded what was done, what was not done, how the individuals spoke, what they said, and how they had expressed themselves using body language. The researchers organized and coded the data, and then they assessed the data via content analysis. Subsequently, themes and patterns were identified. The findings indicated that the children who were continually exposed to the drug environment had learned to be aggressive.

However, there were some limitations in the Dunlap and Johnson (1996) study. First, the study was unique to specific individuals and settings. As a result, the findings cannot necessarily be generalized to other populations and environments. Second, the interpretation of the findings is subjective and is influenced by the personal experiences and expertise of the researchers. To improve the study's credibility, an accumulation of similar case studies will be required. Finally, because the study had a qualitative design, it cannot make numeric predictions.

Second, Freisthler et al. (2017) conducted a quantitative study to determine if there is a relationship between the density of marijuana outlets and violent, property, and marijuana-specific crime. The researchers collected crime data from 481 Census Block Groups over 34 months for both medical and recreational marijuana outlets in Denver, Colorado. The researchers then employed a Bayesian Poisson space-time model to assess the data. As a result, the findings indicated that there is no relationship between marijuana outlets and violent and property crimes in local areas. However, property crimes were displaced to spatially adjacent areas. In addition, the findings indicated that the density of marijuana outlets was related to marijuana-specific crimes in both local and spatially adjacent areas.

However, there were several limitations in the Freisthler et al. (2017) study. First, because the study was an ecological population-level study, the exact social mechanisms related to crime cannot be determined. The sales amount of each marijuana outlet was not considered, and the amount of street marijuana was unavailable. Second, because crime data were provided by the Denver police department, it is possible that the officers manipulated the number of crimes by filing multiple charges for a single event as a way to advocate for more departmental resources. Finally, although the study included spatially-lagged variables, it did not include temporally-lagged variables, which may have affected the model fit.

Finally, Bottorff et al. (2009) conducted an ethnography study to describe the health concerns and problems that motivate some adolescents to consume marijuana for therapeutic reasons and to describe the participants' beliefs about the risks and benefits of using marijuana for therapeutic reasons. The participants included 20 teens who were 13 to 18 years of age who self-identified as using marijuana for therapeutic purposes on a regular basis. The participants lived in British Columbia, Canada, where marijuana was readily available to youths. Thirteen of the participants were male and seven were female. Data were collected via semi-structured interviews, which lasted one to two hours each. A field guide conducted the interviews, the interviews were tape recorded, and field notes, which described the impressions of the participants' responses to the interview questions, were recorded. The field notes were later analyzed by a research team, the interviews were transcribed, and the researchers employed thematic analysis to assess the data. The findings revealed that the teens differentiated themselves from recreational marijuana users because their purpose for using marijuana was to gain relief from difficult feelings (e.g., depression, anxiety, stress, insomnia, physical pain), and they could not find any other way to deal with their problems. In addition, the participants were not concerned about the risks because they believed the amount of marijuana that they consumed was considered normal by social standards.

However, there were several limitations in the Bottorff et al. (2009) study. First, the participants resided in Canada and the findings may not necessarily be generalized to the American population. Second, content analysis is inherently reductive, which may be problematic when dealing with complex texts. Third, qualitative research is dependent upon the experience of the researchers, relevant data must be recognized by the researchers, and the researchers must be able to form bonds with the participants to ensure the participants provide accurate data. Fourth, data analysis for qualitative research depends on the researchers' personal biases and are almost impossible to duplicate. Finally, qualitative analysis does not provide patterns of relationships through numerical representations.

In sum, research studies show that there is a link between environmental factors and personal behaviors. Furthermore, according to the social learning theory, behaviors can be modified via the social environment (Akers & Sellers, 2009). Because public safety is an important social issue, it is important to know if there is a difference between Democrat and Republican jurisdictions and aggressive behaviors of high school students.

III. METHODOLOGY

Political Partisanship Definition

A state was considered either Democrat or Republican based on the U.S. Presidential elections for 2012 and 2016 ("Presidential Voting History by State," n.d.). If a state's electoral college voted for the Democrat U.S. Presidential candidate, then that state was considered a Democrat state. If a state's electoral college voted for the Republican U.S. Presidential candidate, then that state was considered a Republican state. To be considered in this study, a state had to be consistently Democrat or Republican during the years of data collection, which were 2013, 2015, and 2017.

Sample

This study examined electronic second-hand data collected via the Youth Risk Behavior Surveillance System (YRBSS) in 2013, 2015, and 2017 (Kann et al., 2014; Kann et al., 2016; Kann et al., 2018). Data were collected across the U.S. by the Centers for Disease Control and Prevention, which is devoted to the public's safety and health. A three-stage cluster sample design produced a nationally representative sample of male high school students in grades 9–12 who attended public and private schools. The standard questionnaire in 2013 included 86 questions, and the standard questionnaires in 2015 and 2017 included 89 questions.

Statistical Analysis

Because data were collected from the same states for three different times, a certain amount of dependence was expected (Su, 2020). Indeed, a prior study that used the same data source has indicated that the data values are not independent (Davis, 2020). To address this parametric assumption violation, a logistic regression model for repeated measures was fit using a generalized estimating equation (GEE) to answer the research question (Agresti, 2002; Fitzmaurice et al., 2004). In addition, odds ratios (OR) and the 95% confidence interval (CI) were computed to quantify the strength of association between the response variable and the predictor (i.e., political party). A p-value less than 0.05 indicates significance. However, it should be noted that the use of a nonparametric statistic, such as GEE, may result in some loss of efficiency for the estimation of the coefficients relative to the use of a parametric statistic (Fitzmaurice et al., 2004; Su, 2020).

IV. RESULTS

Data were collected from 29 states in 2013, 26 states in 2015, and 25 states in 2017 for a total of 80 observations (see Table 1). Of all the states considered, 61.2% were Republican and 38.8% were Democrat. The mean numbers of males who physically fought at school for the Republican states were 87.95 (SD = 42.62), 88.07 (SD = 59.12), and 69.00 (SD = 31.10) in 2013, 2015, and 2017, respectively (see Table 2). The mean numbers of males who physically fought at school for the Democrat states were 524.10 (SD = 1199.57), 481.09 (SD = 1009.33), and 411.50 (SD = 894.43) in 2013, 2015, and 2017, respectively. The mean rates of males who physically fought at school for the Republican states were 0.118 (SD = 0.027), 0.105 (SD = 0.026), and 0.099 (SD = 0.020) in 2013, 2015, and 2017, respectively. The mean rates of males who physically fought at school for the Democrat states were 0.107 (SD = 0.033), 0.098 (SD = 0.022), and 0.100 (SD = 0.025) in 2013, 2015, and 2017, respectively.

Table 1. Sample Size Overview

Variable	Total number of observations	Number of states (%) per political party		Number of states per year		
		Republican	Democrat	2013	2015	2017
Males who physically fought	80	49 (61.2)	31 (38.8)	29	26	25

Table 2. Descriptive Statistics for the Variables of Interest

Variable	Year	Party	Number of states	Events M	Events SD	Trials M	Trials SD	Events/Trials M	Events/Trials SD	Events/Trials Min	Events/Trials Max
Males who physically fought	2013	R	19	87.95	42.62	765.84	404.93	0.118	0.027	0.075	0.168
		D	10	524.10	1199.57	3511.64	6652.88	0.107	0.033	0.064	0.176
	2015	R	15	88.07	59.12	817.15	437.37	0.105	0.026	0.073	0.169
		D	11	481.09	1009.33	3865.30	6568.23	0.098	0.022	0.071	0.151
	2017	R	15	69.00	31.10	717.63	376.13	0.099	0.020	0.069	0.147
		D	10	411.50	894.43	3251.77	5957.95	0.100	0.025	0.070	0.147
	Overall	R	49	82.18	45.40	766.79	400.11	0.108	0.025	0.069	0.169
		D	31	472.52	1006.69	3553.30	6194.72	0.101	0.026	0.064	0.176

Note: R = Republican; D = Democrat; M = mean; SD = standard deviation; Min = minimum; Max = maximum. Events represent the number of males who physically fought at school. Trials represent the male sample size. Events/Trials represent the rate of males who physically fought at school.

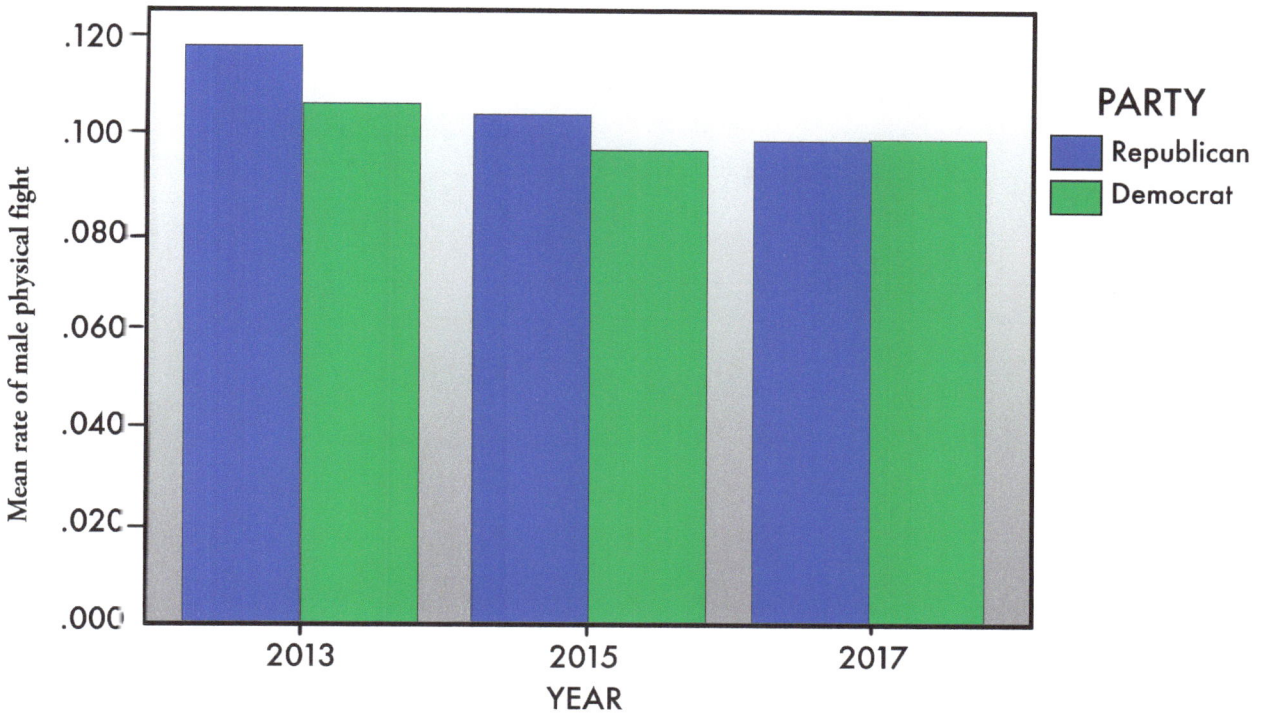

Figure 1. **Bar chart of mean rates of males who physically fought on campus by year and political party.**

Figure 1 provides a direct comparison of the mean rates of male high school students who physically fought on campus for the two political parties. Based on Figure 1, except for 2017, the mean rates of males who physically fight on campus seem to be higher in the Republican states. However, the results of the logistic regression for repeated measures indicate that there is no statistically significant relationship between male high school students who physically fight on campus and political party ($\chi2(1) = 2.728$, p = 0.099, Table 3; OR = 0.783, 95% CI = [0.585, 1.047], Table 4).

Table 3. **Tests of Model Effects**			
Model	Wald χ2	df	p
Males who physically fight on campus	2.728	1	0.099

Note: Wald χ2 = Wald chi-square statistic; df = degrees of freedom; p = p-value.

Table 4. Parameter Estimates and Odds Ratios

Model	Variable	B	SE	95% CI of B		OR	95% CI of OR	
				Lower	Upper		Lower	Upper
Males who physically fight on campus	Intercept	-1.875	0.141	-2.151	-1.598			
	Political Party							
	Republican	-0.025	0.148	-0.536	0.046	0.783	0.585	1.047
	Democrat	Ref						

Note: B = parameter estimate; SE = standard error; CI = confidence interval; lower = lower bound; upper = upper bound; OR = odds ratio; ref = reference group. OR was computed as exp(B).

V. DISCUSSION

The results of the logistic regression for repeated measures indicate that there is no statistically significant relationship between male high school students who physically fight on campus and political party. The results are important because they indicate that neither political party is better than the other when it comes to creating a social learning environment to reduce fights among male high school students. Because the review of the literature indicates that the social learning environment can modify a person's behavior, both political parties may need to consider other ways to modify the social learning environment to achieve the desired results.

Limitations

There were several limitations in this study. First, data were collected only from youth who attended high school and, therefore, are not representative of all persons in this age group (Kann et al., 2016). Second, because the study had a quantitative design, it does not provide an in-depth understanding of the reasons *why* students fight on campus (Berg, 2007). Third, it is not possible to know the actual number of fights on campus because many high school students who are victimized never officially report it to authorities (Loveless, 2020). Fourth, rewards, punishments, and reinforcement, which are central to the social learning theory, are poorly defined (Durkin, 1995). In fact, they are tautological. For example, a person may define something as reinforcing simply because the person finds it reinforcing. Thus, the social learning theory does not provide a true explanation of behavior (Bordens & Abbott, 2008). Fifth, although parametric statistical tests have been systematized, and different tests are simply variations on a central theme, an objection to using nonparametric statistical tests is that they are not systematic (Disha, n.d.). Sixth, when Likert-type scales are used, there is a possibility that the participants may engage in central tendency bias by simply selecting the middle option rather than the best option (Antonovich, 2008). Seventh, participants may alter their behavior if they know that they are being studied. Finally, there are different ways to define political partisanship, which may provide different results. For example, political partisanship may be defined by the political party affiliation of a state's governor or a state's Senate.

REFERENCES

Agresti, A. (2002). *Categorical data analysis.* Hoboken, NJ: John Wiley & Sons, Inc.

Akers, R.L., & Sellers, C. (2009). *Criminological theories: Introduction, evaluation, and application* (5th ed.). New York, NY: Oxford University Press.

Antonovich, M.P. (2008). *Office and SharePoint 2007 user's guide: Integrating SharePoint with Excel, Outlook, Access, and Word.* Berkeley, CA: Apress.

Baier, C.J., & Wright, B.R. (2001). "If you love me, keep my commandments": A meta-analysis of the effect of religion on crime. *Journal of Research in Crime and Delinquency, 38*(1), 3-21. doi:10.1 177/0022427801038001001

Barbour S. (2006). Introduction. In S. Barbour (Ed.), *Writing the critical essay: School violence. An opposing viewpoints guide* (p. 11-16). Detroit, MI: Greenhaven Press.

Berg, B.L. (2007). *Qualitative research methods for the social sciences* (6th ed.). Boston, MA: Pearson Education, Inc.

Blogowska, J., Saroglou, V., & Lambert, C. (2013). Religious prosociality and aggression: It's real. *Journal for the Scientific Study of Religion, 52*(3), 524-536.

Bordens, K., & Abbott, B. (2008). *Research design and methods: A process approach* (7th ed.). Boston, MA: McGraw Hill.

Bottorff, J.L., Johnson, J.L, Moffat, B.M., Mulvogue, T. (2009). Relief-oriented use of marijuana by teens. *Substance Abuse Treatment, Prevention and Policy, 4*, 1-10.

Chew, K. (2016). Bullying means schools are not safe. In Berlatsky (Ed.), *School safety: Opposing viewpoints series* (p. 35-39). Farmington Hills, MI: Greenhaven Press.

Disha, M. (n.d.). *Non-Parametric Tests: Concepts, Precautions and Advantages | Statistics.* https://www.yourarticlelibrary.com/statistics-2/non-parametric-tests-concepts-precautions-and-advantages-statistics/92360

Davis, W.L. (2018). A correlational study of sports participation, religiosity, and verbal aggression among African American female athletes. *Asian Academic Research Journal of Social Science & Humanities, 5*(3), 192-207.

Davis, W.L. (2020). Is There a Difference Between Democrat and Republican States in the Number of Female Students Who Experienced Cyberbullying? *Lincoln Memorial Journal of Social Sciences, 1*(1), Article 1.

Dunlap, E., & Johnson, B. (1996). Aggression and violence in households of crack sellers/abusers. *Applied Behavioral Science Review, 4*(2), 191-217.

Durkin, K. (1995). *Developmental social psychology: From infancy to old age.* Boston, MA: Blackwell Publishing Company.

Fitzmaurice, G. M., Laird, N. M., & Ware, J. H. (2004). *Applied longitudinal analysis.* Hoboken, NJ: John Wiley & Sons.

Freisthler, B., Gaidus, A., Tam, C., Ponicki, W.R., & Gruenewald, P.J. (2017). From medical to recreational marijuana sales: Marijuana outlets and crime in an era of changing marijuana legislation. *Journal of Primary Prevention, 38*, 249-263. doi: 10.1007/s10935-017-0472-9

Jang, S.J., & Johnson, B.R. (2001). Neighborhood disorder, individual religiosity, and adolescent use of illicit drugs: A test of multilevel hypotheses. *Criminology, 39*(1), 109-144.

Kann, L., Kinchen, S., Shanklin, S.L., Flint, K.H., Hawkins, J., Harris, W.A., ... Zaza, S. (2014). Youth risk behavior surveillance—United States, 2013. *Morbidity and Mortality Weekly Report: Surveillance Summaries, 63*(4), 1-172. https://www.cdc.gov/mmwr/pdf/ss/ss6304.pdf

Kann, L., McManus, T., Harris, W.A., Shanklin, S.L., Flint, K.H., Hawkins, ... Zaza, S. (2016). Youth risk behavior surveillance—United States, 2015. *Morbidity and Mortality Weekly Report: Surveillance Summaries, 65*(6), 1-180. https://www.cdc.gov/healthyyouth/data/yrbs/pdf/2015/ss6506_updated.pdf

Kann, L., McManus, T., Harris, W.A., Shanklin, S.L., Flint, K.H., Hawkins, J., Queen, B., ... Ethier, K.A. (2018). Youth risk behavior surveillance—United States, 2017. *Morbidity and Mortality Weekly Report: Surveillance Summaries, 67*(8), 1-479. https://www.cdc.gov/healthyyouth/data/yrbs/pdf/2017/ss6708.pdf

Loveless, B. (2020). Bullying epidemic: Facts, statistics and prevention. *Education Corner.* www.educationcorner.com/bullying-facts-statistics-and-prevention.html

Mattiuzzi, P.G. (2011). Zero tolerance policies are not effective. In N. Merino (Ed.), *School policies: Introducing issues with opposing viewpoints* (p. 62-67). Detroit, MI: Greenhaven Press.

Presidential voting history by state (n.d.). https://ballotpedia.org/Presidential_voting_history_by_state

Snyder, R.L. (2016). *The sport of politics simplified: Democrats versus Republicans, the 2016 spectator's guide.* North Charleston, SC: Createspace.

Su, Y. (2020). *Dr. Su Statistics.* https://sites.google.com/site/drsustat/

Political Partisanship and Male High School Students Who Carry Weapons on School Property

Stephen Church, Lincoln Memorial University (TN)
&
Wayne Davis, Ph.D., Columbia College (SC)

Abstract

Compared to other industrialized countries, America is a relatively violent country. The impact of violent crime on America's youth is alarming and there is no clear solution. School violence is a serious problem that threatens American youth, and politicians are concerned about the high number of violent crimes committed by teens. However, Democrats and Republicans have very different policy platforms on dealing with violent crimes. On the one hand, Republicans support Stand-Your-Ground laws and believe that individuals have a right to protect themselves. On the other hand, Democrats oppose Stand-Your-Ground laws and believe the government is the best source for protecting people. The purpose of this study is to determine if there is a difference between political partisanship and the percentage of male high school students who carry weapons on school property. This study examined electronic second-hand data collected in 2013, 2015, and 2017 by the Centers for Disease Control and Prevention. Data were collected via the Youth Risk Behavior Surveillance System (YRBSS) using a three-stage cluster sample design, which produced a nationally representative sample of students in grades 9-12 who attended public and private schools. The results of logistic regression for repeated measures revealed that there is a statistically significant relationship between male high school students who carry weapons and political party. Males were 56.9% more likely to carry weapons on school property in Republican states than in Democrat states.

I. INTRODUCTION

Compared to other industrialized countries, America is a relatively violent country (Leary, 2008). The impact of violent crime on America's youth is alarming and there is no clear solution. Violent crime causes physical, emotional, and financial trauma for victims and their families. Furthermore, teen victimization has been linked to eating disorders, teen pregnancy, substance abuse, and future violent criminal activity.

School violence is a serious problem that threatens American youth (McCluskey, 2008). First, the amount of crime is underreported because the standards for reporting crimes are inconsistent among the various school districts. Second, the No Child Left Behind Act allows dangerous students to easily transfer from one school to another. Finally, although some school districts have attempted to use zero tolerance policies to reduce student crimes, they have been less than successful and have created hostile and totalitarian learning environments (American Psychology Association Zero Tolerance Task Force, 2008; Casella, 2008; Mukherjee, 2008).

According to the routine activities theory, crime occurs when three factors converge: a motivated offender, a suitable target, and the absence of a capable guardian (Williams & McShane, 2013). This is important because the availability of weapons may either encourage or discourage crime. For example, if weapons are readily available, they might provide the motivation needed for a person to commit a crime. On the other hand, if weapons are readily availability, the potential target may be armed, which may discourage crime. The Democrats support the idea that the removal of weapons from society will reduce the motivation to commit crime, which will promote a peaceful society (Snyder, 2016). The Republicans support the idea that the possession of weapons by individuals will discourage crime, which will promote a peaceful society. Thus, it comes down to whether the residents believe that other individuals will willfully comply with the government's request not to carry weapons or whether they feel that they can only trust themselves for their own personal safety. This argument is complicated by the fact that the police are required to protect society as a whole, but they are not required to necessarily protect specific individuals (Del Carmen & Hemmens, 2017).

Politicians are concerned about the high number of violent crimes committed by teens (Barbour, 1999). Democrats and Republicans have very different policy platforms, and they fight for power to ensure that their policies are implemented (Snyder, 2016). On the one hand, Republicans believe that individuals have a right to protect themselves and they support Stand-Your-Ground laws. On the other hand, Democrats oppose the possession of weapons and Stand-Your-Ground laws because they believe civilians should not take the law into their own hands. If the government reflects the people whom it serves, students in Republican states are expected to carry more weapons than students in Democrat states. The purpose of this study was to determine if there is a difference between political partisanship and the percentage of male students in grades 9-12 who carry weapons on school property. The research question and the null hypothesis are listed below.

Research Question: Is there a difference between Democrat and Republican states in the percentage of male high school students who carry weapons on school property?

Null Hypothesis: There is no difference between Democrat and Republican states in the percentage of male high school students who carry weapons on school property.

II. LITERATURE REVIEW

Democrats and Republicans have different views on weapon-control policies (Snyder, 2016). A review of the literature will investigate whether weapon-control policies impact weapon-related crime. Republicans argue that criminals will be less likely to attack potential victims who may be armed. In this case, by making themselves less suitable targets, individuals may discourage crime. Democrats argue that the availability of weapons increases the likelihood for violent crime. In this case, readily available weapons may be the motivation needed for persons to commit crimes. Because high school students cannot legally carry weapons on campus, literature on the subject matter is sparse. Therefore, studies related to the subject matter that involve adults will be reviewed.

First, Doucette et al. (2019) employed a longitudinal method study to examine the association between right-to-carry firearm laws and firearm workplace homicides using data collected from 1992 to 2017 in a 50-state panel. During the study, the researchers employed 1) a pooled, cross-sectional, time-series analysis to examine the average effect and 2) a random effects meta-analysis to examine the state-specific effect. The researchers then used a generalized linear mixed model with negative binomial distribution to assess the data, and the findings indicated that the right-to-carry firearms was positively related to a higher number of firearm workplace homicides.

However, there were several limitations in the Doucette et al. (2019) study. Due to nature of the Census of Fatal Occupational Injuries, the total population analysis likely underestimated the true incidence of firearm workplace homicides. The Census of Fatal Occupational Injuries only provided data on employees and not on non-employees who were killed during a workplace homicide event, which underestimated the true count. In addition, the Census of Fatal Occupational Injuries did not provide information on lifestyles or work conditions, which may have affected the number of workplace homicides. Finally, due to the rules involving the Census of Fatal Occupational Injuries, data that were necessary to perform an important sensitivity analysis that involved non-firearm workplace homicides were unavailable.

Second, Webster et al. (2014) conducted a quasi-experimental study to assess the relationship between the 2007 repeal of Missouri's permit-to-purchase gun law, which required all handgun purchasers to pass a background check, and the number of homicides in the state. The researchers used the Centers for Disease Control and Prevention's state-level gun-related homicide rates collected annually from 1999 to 2012. The researchers used t-tests to compare the homicide rates before and after the law was repealed. The findings indicated that the repeal of Missouri's permit-to-purchase handgun licensing law was positively related to the number of homicides in the state.

However, there were several limitations in the Webster et al. (2014) study. First, because Missouri passed a Stand-Your-Ground law at the same time the permit-to-purchase law was repealed, there is a threat to the validity of the study's findings. Second, the pre-repeal baseline period was relatively short, and a longitudinal study would be required to observe incremental changes in the dependent variable over a long period of time. Third, the study was conducted in Missouri and the findings cannot necessarily be generalized to other states. Finally, because the study was quantitative in nature, it cannot determine the motives behind the behaviors.

Third, Swanson et al. (2016) conducted a quasi-experimental study to examine if firearm laws are effective in preventing individuals with serious mental illness from committing gun-related violent crimes and gun-related suicide. The researchers collected data from 81,704 adults who were receiving mental health services from the public behavioral health systems in two large countries in Florida from 2002 to 2011. The researchers employed regression analysis and difference in differences to assess the data. Although the findings indicated that violent crime decreased after the implementation of gun laws, there was no relationship when only violent gun-related crimes were considered. In addition, the findings indicated that mentally ill individuals who were already disqualified from legally carrying handguns were more likely than the general public to commit gun-related suicide, but they were not more likely to commit gun-related homicide.

However, there were several limitations in the Swanson et al. (2016) study. First, the measure of whether guns were or were not used during violent crimes was imprecise. Thus, if the data were imprecise, then the findings may be imprecise. Second, most of the individuals arrested for violent crimes were already legally prohibited from carrying firearms. Thus, it is unclear if the gun-control laws had any impact on the number of violent gun-related crimes. Third, because many of the individuals with serious mental illness live in poverty and are socially isolated, they may not be able to readily obtain guns. In other words, even if they wanted to commit gun-related crimes, they may not be able to commit them, independent of the law. Finally, because the study was quantitative in nature, it does not provide an in-depth understanding of the meanings that the participants have associated with their lived experiences (Berg, 2007).

Fourth, Kwon et al. (1997) conducted a quantitative study to evaluate the relationship between gun-control laws adopted by states and municipalities and gun-related deaths. States were divided into two groups: 26 states had some type of gun-control restrictions (e.g., licenses, waiting periods, etc.) and 24 states that had no gun-control restrictions. Because poverty level, unemployment rate, and alcohol consumption have been linked to violence in the past, these variables were also considered. The researchers collected data for 1990 from several different sources. The firearm death rates were collected from the National Center for Health Statistics. Poverty rates, unemployment rates, and population densities were collected from the Statistical Abstract of the United States. Data for alcohol consumption were collected from the Eighth Special Report to the U.S. Congress on Alcohol and Health. The researchers used multivariate regression to assess the data, and the findings indicated that the relationship between gun-control laws and gun-related deaths was not statistically significant. However, the findings indicated that poverty level, unemployment rate, and alcohol consumption were related to firearm deaths.

However, there were several limitations in the Kwon et al. (1997) study. First, many of the gun-control laws have changed since 1990, which make the findings less than applicable to today's environments. Second, multivariate analysis requires a larger sample of data for more meaningful results. Otherwise, there may be high standard errors. Finally, because the study was quantitative in nature, it investigated *how* variables were numerically related (i.e., the modus operandi), but it did not investigate *why* variables were related (i.e., the motive).

Finally, Gius (2017) conducted a quantitative study to determine if permit-to-purchase firearm laws are related to the number of firearm homicides. The researcher used state-level longitudinal data collected from all 50 states from 1980 to 2011. The number of homicides was obtained from the Supplementary Homicide Reports, which were provided by the Bureau of Justice Statistics. Data on permit-to-purchase were obtained from 1) the Giffords Law Center to Prevent Gun Violence (2013), 2) Ludwig and Cook (2003), and 3) Rudolph et al. (2015). The researcher used a fixed effects regression model on the data to control for both state and year effects. The findings indicated that permit-to-purchase firearm laws had no significant effect on the number of state-level firearm homicides.

However, there were several limitations in the Gius (2017) study. First, only murder was examined. Guns are used in a variety of other crimes, such as robbery and rape, but these crimes were not considered. Second, because several states have significantly altered their gun laws since 2011, new and more current data may result in different findings. Finally, because the study was quantitative in nature, it failed to provide the meanings and motivations behind the individuals' behaviors.

In sum, to reduce violence, some of the studies support gun-control policies and some do not. In terms of political parties, it is unclear which political party philosophy is better in reducing weapon-related crimes. According to the routine activities theory, motivated criminals seek suitable targets who are not well protected (Williams & McShane, 2018). If residents are authorized to carry weapons (i.e., the Republican party's position), then they may become less suitable targets for crime. However, if strict weapon-control policies are in place (i.e., the Democrat party's position), then potential criminals may not have the motivation nor opportunity to commit crime.

III. METHODOLOGY

Political Partisanship Definition

A state was considered either Democrat or Republican based on the color assigned to that state during U.S. Presidential elections (2012 and 2016). If a state's electoral college voted for the Democrat U.S. Presidential candidate, then that state was considered a blue state ("Presidential Voting History by State," n.d.). If a state's electoral college voted for the Republican U.S. Presidential candidate, then that state was considered a red state. To be considered in this study, a state had to be consistently red or blue during the years of data collection, which were 2013, 2015, and 2017.

Data

This study examined electronic government-based second-hand data collected across the U.S. in 2013, 2015, and 2017 by the Centers for Disease Control and Prevention, which is devoted to the public's safety and health (Kann et al., 2014; Kann et al., 2016; Kann et al., 2018). Data were collected via the Youth Risk Behavior Surveillance System (YRBSS) using a three-stage cluster sample design, which produced a nationally representative sample of male students in grades 9-12 who attended public and private schools. The standard questionnaire in 2013 included 86 questions, and the standard questionnaires in 2015 and 2017 included 89 questions.

Statistical Analysis

Because the data in 2013, 2015, and 2017 were collected from the same states, a certain amount of correlation/dependence was expected (Su, 2020). Indeed, this was indicated in a prior study that used Poisson regression on data collected from the same surveys, which resulted in a very large overdisperson problem (Davis, 2020). Thus, in order to address this parametric assumption violation, a logistic regression model for repeated measures was fit using a generalized estimating equation (GEE) to answer the research question (Agresti, 2002; Fitzmaurice et al., 2004). In addition, odds ratios (OR) and the 95% confidence interval (CI) were computed to quantify the strength of association between the response variable and the predictor (i.e., political party). A p-value less than 0.05 indicates significance. However, it should be noted that although GEE avoids the distributional assumptions of independent observations, the use of a nonparametric statistic (e.g., GEE) may result in some loss of efficiency for the estimation of the coefficients relative to the optimal likelihood-based estimates when distributional assumptions are satisfied (Fitzmaurice et al., 2004; Su, 2020).

IV. RESULTS

Data were collected from 29 states in 2013, 27 states in 2015, and 28 states in 2017 for a total of 84 observations (see Table 1). Of all the states considered, 56% were Republican and 44% were Democrat. The mean numbers of males carrying weapons at school for the Republican states were 77.89 (SD = 73.19), 74.87 (SD = 62.84), and 65.00 (SD = 53.26) in 2013, 2015, and 2017, respectively (see Table 2). The mean numbers of males carrying weapons at school for the Democrat states were 222.64 (SD = 408.90), 199.25 (SD = 341.38), and 224.50 (SD = 477.96) in 2013, 2015, and 2017, respectively. The mean rates of males carrying weapons at school for the Republican states were 0.094 (SD = 0.028), 0.096 (SD = 0.030), and 0.089 (SD = 0.029) in 2013, 2015, and 2017, respectively. The mean rates of males carrying weapons at school for the Democrat states were 0.065 (SD = 0.021), 0.059 (SD = 0.016), and 0.062 (SD = 0.015) in 2013, 2015, and 2017, respectively.

Table 1. Sample Size Overview

Variable	Total number of states	Number of states (%) per political party		Number of states per year		
		Republican	Democrat	2013	2015	2017
Males carrying weapons	84	47 (56.0)	37 (44.0)	29	27	28

Table 2. Descriptive Statistics for the Variables of Interest

Variable	Year	Party	Number of states	Events		Trials		Events/Trials			
				M	SD	M	SD	M	SD	Min	Max
Males carrying weapons	2013	R	18	77.89	73.19	754.56	425.21	0.094	0.028	0.049	0.150
		D	11	222.64	408.90	3354.91	6362.94	0.065	0.021	0.040	0.103
	2015	R	15	74.87	62.84	730.27	358.07	0.096	0.030	0.040	0.155
		D	12	199.25	341.38	3450.92	6301.80	0.059	0.016	0.037	0.086
	2017	R	14	65.00	53.26	693.00	389.98	0.089	0.029	0.042	0.142
		D	14	224.50	477.96	3000.93	5071.72	0.062	0.015	0.045	0.093
	Overall	R	47	73.09	63.35	728.47	386.61	0.093	0.028	0.040	0.155
		D	37	215.76	405.81	3252.11	5719.30	0.062	0.017	0.037	0.103

Note: R = Republican; D = Democrat; M = mean; SD = standard deviation; Min = minimum; Max = maximum. Events represent the number of males carrying weapons at school. Trials represent the male sample size. Events/Trials represent the rate of males carrying weapons at school.

Figure 1 shows the bar chart of mean rates of males carrying weapons by year and political party, which provides a direct comparison of the mean rates of males carrying weapons at school between the two political parties. Based on Figure 1, Republican states seem to have higher mean rates of males carrying weapons at school than Democrat states. Furthermore, the results of the logistic regression for repeated measures indicate that there is a statistically significant relationship between males carrying weapons and political party ($\chi2(1) = 17.728$, $p < 0.001$, Table 3). In particular, males were 56.9% more likely to carry weapons at school in Republican states than in Democrat states (OR = 1.569, 95% CI = [1.272, 1.936], Table 4).

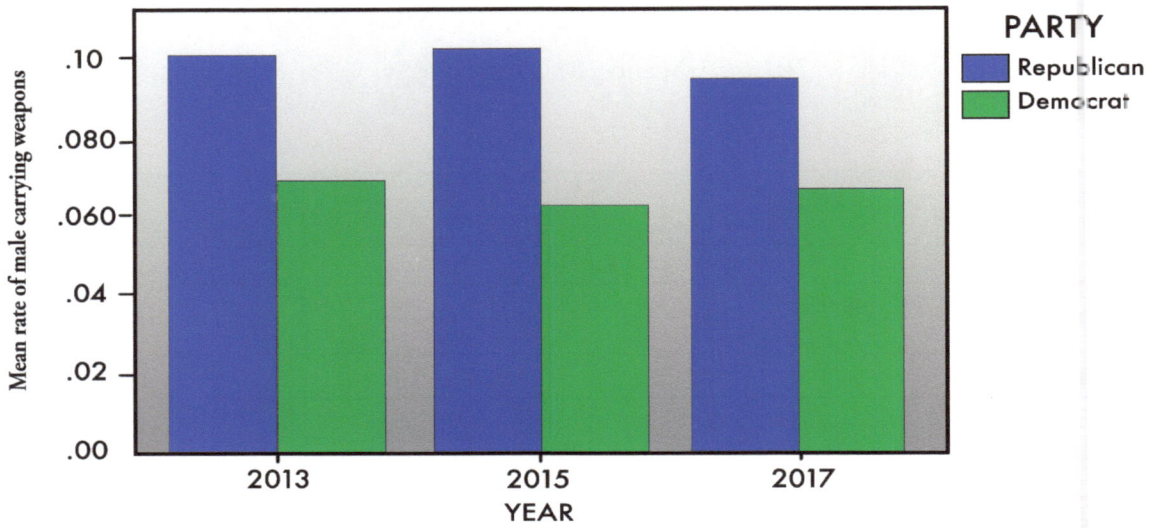

Figure 1. **Bar chart of mean rates of males carrying weapons at school by year and political party.**

Table 3. **Tests of Model Effects**			
Model	Wald $\chi2$	df	p
Males carrying weapons	17.728	1	< 0.001

Note: Wald $\chi2$ = Wald chi-square statistic; df = degrees of freedom; p = p-value.

Table 4. **Parameter Estimates and Odds Ratios**								
Model	Variable	B	SE	95% CI of B		OR	95% CI of OR	
				Lower	Upper		Lower	Upper
Males carrying weapons	Intercept	-2.644	0.048	-2.738	-2.551			
	Political Party							
	Republican	0.451	0.107	0.241	0.660	1.569	1.272	1.936
	Democrat	Ref						

Note: B = parameter estimate; SE = standard error; CI = confidence interval; lower = lower bound; upper = upper bound; OR = odds ratio; ref = reference group. OR was computed as exp(B).

V. DISCUSSION

The results of the logistic regression for repeated measures indicate that there is a statistically significant relationship between male high school students who carry weapons on campus and political party. Males were 56.9% more likely to carry weapons at school in Republican states than in Democrat states. The results are important because they may indicate that youths in Republican states do not have confidence that the government will protect them, and/or they are taking advantage of the Republican party's stance on Stand-Your-Ground laws and weapons-control policies. The results may also indicate that youths in Democrat states do have confidence that the government will protect them, and, therefore, they do not feel the need to arm themselves. Although policies from either political party do not authorize high school students to carry weapons on campus, male high school students seem to reflect the philosophies of their respective state's political party.

Limitations

There were several limitations in the current study. First, because the sample was limited to male students in grades 9-12, the findings cannot be generalized to other populations. Second, because the data used in the study were second-hand and collected for a different reason, the data values cannot be more clearly defined. Third, because Likert-type scales were used to collect data, there is a possibility that the participants were forced to select options that did not accurately represent their realities (Antonovich, 2008). Fourth, not all states and large urban school districts, which provided data, included all of the standard questions on their Youth Risk Behavior Surveillance questionnaires (Kann et al, 2016). Fifth, for the routine activities theory, the level of motivation is not well defined (Williams & McShane, 2018). Finally, because the study was quantitative in nature, it does not provide an in-depth understanding of *why* male high school students carried weapons on campus (Berg, 2007).

REFERENCES

Agresti, A. (2002). *Categorical data analysis*. Hoboken, NJ: John Wiley & Sons, Inc.

American Psychological Association Zero Tolerance Task Force (2008). Zero tolerance policies are ineffective and harsh. In J. Carroll (Ed.), *Opposing viewpoint series: School policies* (p. 38-47). Detroit, MI: Greenhaven Press.

Antonovich, M.P. (2008). *Office and SharePoint 2007 user's guide: Integrating SharePoint with Excel, Outlook, Access, and Word*. Berkeley, CA: Apress.

Barbour, S. (1999). Introduction. In S. Barbour (Ed.), *Opposing viewpoints digests: Teen violence* (p. 8-23). San Diego, CA: Greenhaven Press.

Berg, B. (2007). *Qualitative research methods for the social sciences* (6th ed.). Boston, MA: Pearson Education, Inc.

Casella, R. (2008). School surveillance technology is totalitarian. In J. Carroll (Ed.), *Opposing viewpoint series: School policies* (p. 90-99). Detroit, MI: Greenhaven Press.

Davis, W.L. (2020). Is There a Difference Between Democrat and Republican States in the Number of Female Students Who Experienced Cyberbullying? *Lincoln Memorial Journal of Social Sciences, 1*(1), Article 1.

Del Carmen. & Hemmens, C. (2017). *Criminal procedures: Laws & practice* (10th ed). Boston, MA: Cengage.

Doucette, M., Crifasi, C.K., & Frattaroli, S. (2019). Right-to-carry laws and firearm workplace homicides: A longitudinal analysis (1992-2017). *American Journal of Public Health, 109*(12), 1747-1753. doi: 10.2105/AJPH.2019.305307

Fitzmaurice, G. M., Laird, N. M., & Ware, J. H. (2004). *Applied longitudinal analysis*. Hoboken, NJ: John Wiley & Sons.

Giffords Law Center to Prevent Gun Violence (2013). www.smartgunlaws.org.

Gius, M. (2017). Effects of permit-to-purchase laws on state-level firearm murder rates. *Atlantic Economic Journal, 45*(1), 73-80. doi: 10.1007/s11293-016-9529-z

Kann, L., Kinchen, S., Shanklin, S.L., Flint, K.H., Hawkins, J., Harris, W.A., . . . Zaza, S. (2014). Youth risk behavior surveillance—United States, 2013. *Morbidity and Mortality Weekly Report: Surveillance Summaries, 63*(4), 1-172. https://www.cdc.gov/mmwr/pdf/ss/ss6304.pdf

Kann, L., McManus, T., Harris, W.A., Shanklin, S.L., Flint, K.H., Hawkins, . . . Zaza, S. (2016). Youth risk behavior surveillance—United States, 2015. *Morbidity and Mortality Weekly Report: Surveillance Summaries, 65*(6), 1-180. https://www.cdc.gov/healthyyouth/data/yrbs/pdf/2015/ss6506_updated.pdf

Kann, L., McManus, T., Harris, W.A., Shanklin, S.L., Flint, K.H., Hawkins, J., Queen, B., . . . Ethier, K.A. (2018). Youth risk behavior surveillance—United States, 2017. *Morbidity and Mortality Weekly Report: Surveillance Summaries, 67*(8), 1-479. https://www.cdc.gov/healthyyouth/data/yrbs/pdf/2017/ss6708.pdf

Kwon, I. G., Scott, B., Safranski, S.R., & Bae, M. (1997). The effectiveness of gun control laws: Multivariate statistical analysis. *American Journal of Economics and Sociology, 56*(1), 41-50.

Leary, M.L. (2008). Violent crime is a serious problem. In L. Gerdes (Ed.), *Opposing viewpoint series: Violence* (p. 21-26). Detroit, MI: Greenhaven Press.

Ludwig, J., & Cook, P. (Eds.) (2003). *Evaluating gun policy: Effects on crime and violence.* Washington: The Brookings Institution.

McCluskey, N. (2008). School violence threatens American youth. In L. Gerdes (Ed.), *Opposing viewpoint series: Violence* (p. 36-41). Detroit, MI: Greenhaven Press.

Mukherjee, E. (2008). Metal detectors create a hostile learning environment. In J. Carroll (Ed.), *Opposing viewpoint series: School policies* (p. 74-81). Detroit, MI: Greenhaven Press.

Presidential voting history by state (n.d.). https://ballotpedia.org/Presidential_voting_ history_by_state

Rudolph, K., Stuart, E., Vernick, J., & Webster, D. (2015). Association between Connecticut's permit-to-purchase handgun law and homicides. *American Journal of Public Health, 105*(8). e49-e54.

Snyder, R.L. (2016). *The sport of politics simplified: Democrats versus Republicans, the 2016 spectator's guide.* North Charleston, SC: Createspace

Su, Y. (2020). *Dr. Su Statistics.* https://sites.google.com/site/drsustat/

Swanson, J.W., Easter, M.M., Robertson, A.G., Swartz, M.S., Alanis-Hirsch, K., Moseley, D., ... Petrila, J. (2016). Gun violence, mental illness, and laws that prohibit gun possession: Evidence from two Florida counties. *Health Affairs, 35*(6), 1067-1075.

Webster, D., Crifasi, C.K., & Vernick, J.S. (2014). Effects of the repeal of Missouri's handgun purchaser licensing law on homicides. *Journal of Urban Health, 91*(2), 293-302. doi: 10.1007/s11524-014-9865-8

Williams, F.P., & McShane, M.D. (2018). *Criminological theory* (7th ed.). New York, NY: Pearson.

Political Partisanship and Male High School Students Who Carry Handguns

John Page, Lincoln Memorial University (TN)
&
Wayne L. Davis, Ph.D., Columbia College (SC)

Abstract

Handguns play a significant role in criminal activity. About 66% of all murders and 40% of robberies involve firearms. Because there are about than 470 residents for each full-time police officer in America, the police cannot effectively protect individual citizens. According to the differential association theory, criminality is a product of shared values, motives, drives, rationalizations, and attitudes that can be influenced by perceptions of the legal code. Democrats and Republicans have different views on reducing social harm via gun-control legal codes, and each political party creates its own unique ambience. Indeed, because each political party believes that its gun-control platform is best, it is important to know how children are responding to the issue in each political partisanship jurisdiction. Because gun-related research is essential for public safety, and because funding for gun violence research comprises less than 0.1% of the Centers for Disease Control and Prevention's annual budget, additional research is important for better understanding the issue. Therefore, the purpose of this study was to determine if there is a difference between Democrat and Republican states in the percentage of male high school students who carry handguns in their respective jurisdictions. This study examined electronic second-hand data collected in 2013, 2015, and 2017 by the Centers for Disease Control and Prevention. The results of logistic regression for repeated measures indicate that there is a statistically significant relationship between male high school students who carry handguns and political party. Male high school students were 77.4% more likely to carry handguns in Republican states than in Democrat states.

I. INTRODUCTION

Handguns play a significant role in criminal activity (Siegel, 2018). About 66% of all murders and 40% of robberies involve firearms. Because there are about than 470 residents for each full-time police officer in America, the police cannot effectively protect individual citizens (Duffin, 2020; United States Census Bureau, 2020). In 2016, for example, there were 56,347 deaths due to gun violence (Gun Violence Achieve, 2020). In 2017, there were 59,289 deaths due to gun violence. In 2018, there were 55,192 deaths due to gun violence. International criminologists have argued that the high rate of lethal violence caused with handguns clearly separates the U.S. from other developed countries in a bad way. In short, it is risky to depend on the police to protect a person's life.

There is an on-going debate over the possession of handguns in America. On the one hand, some individuals believe that self-protection is the best way to defend oneself against criminal attacks (Siegel, 2018). Each year, tens of thousands of victims use guns for self-defense (Kleck & Gertz, 1995). Indeed, a study of 27,000 crime cases has indicated that the possession of handguns was better in reducing the likelihood of property loss and injury when compared to nonresistance, without contributing to injury in any meaningful way. Furthermore, most of 1,615 felons who were interviewed in a survey stated that they were more afraid of armed victims than of police (Wright & Rossi, 1985). On the other hand, some individuals argue that as the number of guns increases, so does the number of gun-related crimes (Siegel, 2018). In other words, if guns are available, they will be used. Surveys of high school students indicate that six to ten percent of students have carried handguns in the past, and when individuals carry handguns, the seriousness of their crimes increases. Handguns are dangerous weapons when they fall into the hands of irresponsible individuals, such as youths, and, as a result, schoolyard fights may turn into homicides.

When police officers were surveyed and asked whether they believed banning the ownership of all firearms would reduce and prevent gun-related crime, 97% of the officers stated that they felt criminals would still obtain guns for criminal use (Thobaben et al., 1991). Because there are so many guns in the U.S., it would be very difficult, if not impossible, to keep the guns out of private hands, whether the individuals were criminals or not. It is estimated that about 33% of American households contain guns (Siegel, 2018). Even Sweden, which has some of the strictest gun laws in the world, still experiences significant gun-related violence (Khoshnood, 2019).

Democrats and Republicans have different views on gun-control policies, and each political party creates its own unique ambience (Pearson-Merkowitz & Dyck, 2017; Snyder, 2016). According to the differential association theory, criminality is a product of shared values, motives, drives, rationalizations, and attitudes that can be influenced by perceptions of the legal code (Siegel, 2018; Williams & McShane,

2018). By interacting and communicating with other people, an individual will learn the definitions of acceptable behaviors, which can be reinforced by the frequency, duration, priority, and intensity of the experiences. Democrats support gun control laws that restrict gun ownership because they feel that the availability of guns will lead to gun violence (Snyder, 2016). The Republicans, on the other hand, feel that law-abiding individuals have the right to possess handguns to protect themselves and their families. In addition, gun ownership provides some protection against the government from completely taking over their lives. Because gun-related research is essential for public safety, and because funding for gun violence research comprises less than 0.1% of the Centers for Disease Control and Prevention's annual budget, additional research is important for better understanding the issue (Rajan et al., 2018). Indeed, because each political party believes that its gun-control platform is best, it is important to know how children are responding to the issue in each political partisanship jurisdiction. The research question and the null hypothesis are listed below.

Research Question: Is there a difference between Democrat and Republican states in the percentage of male high school students who carry handguns?

Null Hypothesis: There is no difference between Democrat and Republican states in the percentage of male high school students who carry handguns.

II. LITERATURE REVIEW

First, Lemieux (2014) conducted a quantitative study to examine if gun violence and mass shootings are a cultural artifact and if gun violence and mass shootings are more prevalent due to lax gun control regulations. The researcher used a three-level, cross-sectional approach. The macro level compared 25 developed countries based on military expenditures and movies that glorified the use of guns; the meso level compared all 50 states in America by using data collected from the Uniform Crime Report; and the micro level compared 73 public mass shootings that occurred in the U.S. from 1983 to 2013. The researcher used multivariate analysis to assess the data, and the findings indicated that gun control legislation reduced overall fatalities related to firearms for both national and international territories. In other words, the best predictor of firearm deaths was the number of guns owned by civilians. However, except for the Southern region of the U.S., there was no correlation between the gun culture and the occurrence of mass shootings. In addition, 71% of the guns used in the mass shootings were legally and directly accessible to the killers, and 56% of the shooters had been diagnosed with a mental illness.

However, there were several limitations in the Lemieux (2014) study. Due to the low number of mass shootings in countries other than the U.S., there is an insufficient amount of data in the other countries for effective quantitative analysis. Second, the data analysis failed to capture the evaluation of state laws over time and did not take into account the gun laws that were in place at the times of the shootings. Finally, because of the variables' ambiguous temporal precedence, the findings cannot indicate causal relationships.

Second, Jehan et al. (2018) conducted a quantitative study to determine the relationship between firearm laws and firearm-related injuries across the United States. Data were collected from the 2011 Nationwide Inpatient Sample database on 2,583 firearm-related victims from 44 states. States were placed into one of two groups based on whether the state had strict firearm laws or non-strict firearm laws based on the Brady Center score. Ten states were classified as having strict firearm laws and 34 states were classified as having non-strict firearm laws. The researchers conducted linear regression and correlation analysis on the data, and the findings indicated that states with non-strict firearm laws had a greater number of firearm victims.

However, there were several limitations in the Jehan et al. (2018) study. First, the 2011 Nationwide Inpatient Sample dataset represented a 20% sample of all inpatient discharges, which were weighted to represent national estimates and not state estimates. Second, the data did not consider victims who died due to firearm injuries before they reached the hospital. Finally, the differences in the implementation of firearm-related laws across the states were not considered.

Third, Ludwig and Cook (2000) conducted a study to determine if the Brady Act is related to a reduction in gun-related homicides and gun-related suicides. The Brady Act requires licensed firearm dealers to observe a waiting period and to perform background checks on potential customers before the dealers sell firearms. The researchers collected data on homicides, gun-related homicides, suicides, and gun-related suicides from the National Center for Health Statistics from 1985 to 1997. The researchers used weighted linear regression and negative binomial regression to assess the data. The findings indicated that the implementation of the Brady Act had no effect on the number of homicides, gun-related homicides, or overall suicide rates. However, the implementation of the Brady Act did reduce firearm suicides for persons 55 years of age or older.

However, there were several limitations in the Ludwig and Cook (2000) study. First, the reliability of the study's findings is questionable because it is unclear how many guns moved into secondary markets due to the Brady Act. Second, because the data used in the study were secondary data, the data values cannot be more clearly defined. Finally, because the study was quantitative in nature, it investigated *how* variables were numerically related but not *why* the variables were related.

Fourth, Siegel and Boine (2019) conducted a quantitative study to determine if there was a relationship between eight major types of firearms laws and firearm-related homicide rates. The eight types of firearm laws in four categories included laws that regulated 1) who may purchase and possess firearms, 2) the types of firearms and ammunition allowed, 3) when firearms may be used, and 4) the reasons why firearms may be purchased. Data were collected over a 20-year period from 1997 to 2016 for all 50 states for a total of 1,000 observations. The researchers used a panel regression model to evaluate the change in the overall homicide rate in a given state in a given year in relation to changes in the presence of a state law. The findings indicated that laws that regulated the types of guns and ammunition that individuals may possess did not affect the overall homicide rate. However, the number of laws that regulated who may possess such firearms was inversely related to the number of firearm homicides. In short, regulating who may possess firearms had a greater impact on homicide rates than regulating the types of firearms that were allowed in society.

However, there were several limitations in the Siegel and Boine (2019) study. First, although the researchers took steps to help establish evidence for causal relationships, the study can only claim to show correlational relationships. Second, there was inadequate power to evaluate several of the laws in several of the states because the laws were not enacted before the data were collected. Finally, because the study only considered broad, population-based outcomes, the study may not have adequate power to detect narrowly crafted laws expected to affect certain subpopulations.

Fifth, Loftin and McDowall (1984) conducted a study to determine the impact of a mandatory sentence gun law on violent crimes, such as battery, robbery, and homicide. The researchers used an interrupted time-series design, which was applied to Miami, Jacksonville, and Tampa. These cities were chosen because they were three of the largest cities in the state, they were geographically separated and demographically distinct, and they accounted for at least 33% of the total number of violent crimes in Florida. To enhance the study's validity, the researchers used a control series for each analysis to reduce historical threats and an Autoregressive Integrated Moving Average noise model to control for the effects of nonstationarity and autocorrelation. In addition, the researchers employed an intervention model to represent the effects of the gun law. For each series, three types of intervention models were considered, which were an abrupt permanent change model, a gradual permanent change model, and an abrupt temporary change model. The findings of the intervention analysis indicated that the Florida gun law did not reduce violent crime.

However, there were several limitations in the Loftin and McDowall (1984) study. First, it is possible that other events, which occurred at about the same time as the intervention, were actually responsible for the observed changes. Second, the study was conducted in Florida, which may not necessarily represent other state populations. Finally, because the study was quantitative in nature, it does not provide an in-depth understanding of the motives behind the participants' actions (Berg, 2007).

Finally, Lott and Whitley (2001) conducted a study on state level data to assess the relationship between safe-storage gun laws and the number of violent crimes, the number of accidental gun deaths, and the number of suicides committed with guns. The data for the crime rates were collected from 1977 to 1996, and the data for the accidental deaths and suicides were collected from 1979 to 1996. The researchers employed regressions with weighted tobits to adjust for each state's population. The findings indicated that there was a positive relationship between safe-storage gun laws and the number of rapes, robberies, and burglaries. The findings seem to indicate that the safe-storage gun laws impaired people's ability to access their guns when they were needed for self-defense. The study's findings also indicated that there was no relationship between safe-storage gun laws and reduced juvenile accidental gun deaths or suicides. It appears that the accidental shootings involved gun owners who disregarded safe-storage laws. In addition, when guns were not available, juveniles found other means to commit suicide.

However, there were several limitations in the Lott and Whitley (2001) study. First, it is possible that safe-storage gun laws have no effect on people's behaviors in storing guns. It is assumed that the laws modified people's behaviors. Second, if safe-gun storage laws did alter people's behaviors, they may have affected only those individuals who were already at a low risk of accidental shootings or suicides. Because these individuals were already at a low risk, the laws may not have affected this particular group. Finally, because the study was quantitative in nature, it cannot provide a deep understanding of experiences that is needed to uncover hidden phenomena (Hatch, 2002).

In sum, the studies are mixed. Some studies indicate that strict gun-control policies may reduce social harm, and other studies indicate that strict gun-control policies may increase social harm. It is difficult to say how the social learning environment, as created by the political parties, may impact the behaviors of male high school students.

III. METHODOLOGY

Political Partisanship Definition

A state was considered either Democrat or Republican based on U.S. Presidential elections in 2012 and 2016 ("Presidential Voting History by State," n.d.). If a state's electoral college voted for the Democrat U.S. Presidential candidate, then that state was considered a Democrat state. If a state's electoral college voted for the Republican U.S. Presidential candidate, then that state was considered a Republican state. To be considered in this study, a state had to be consistently Democrat or Republican during the years of data collection, which were 2013, 2015, and 2017.

Data

This study analyzed secondary data, which were collected by the Centers for Disease Control and Prevention (Kann et al., 2014; Kann et al., 2016; Kann et al., 2018). The Centers for Disease Control and Prevention provided Youth Risk Behavior Surveillance System questionnaires in 2013, 2015, and 2017 to high school students in grades 9-12, who attended public and private schools across America. The standard questionnaire in 2013 included 86 questions, and the standard questionnaires in 2015 and 2017 included 89 questions. A three-stage cluster sample design was used, which produced a nationally representative sample of male high school students.

Statistical Analysis

Because data were collected in 2013, 2015, and 2017 from the same states, there is the possibility that the same students may have responded to more than one survey during their four years of high school attendance (Kann et al., 2014; Kann et al., 2016; Kann et al., 2018). Therefore, a certain amount of correlation among the data values was expected (Su, 2020). This could be problematic if researchers decided to use a parametric statistic to assess the data. Indeed, a prior study that used Poisson regression to assess data collected from the same surveys ran into a huge overdisperson problem (Davis, 2020). To address this overdispersion problem, the current study used a generalized estimating equation (GEE), which is a nonparametric statistic, to assess the data. However, relative to the use of a parametric statistic, the use of a nonparametric statistic may result in some loss of efficiency for the estimation of the coefficients (Fitzmaurice et al., 2004; Su, 2020).

IV. RESULTS

Data were collected from 24 states in 2013, 15 states in 2015, and 17 states in 2017 for a total of 56 observations (see Table 1). Of all the states considered, 60.7% were Republican and 39.3% were Democrat. The mean numbers of male high school students who carried handguns for the Republican states were 109.53 (SD = 83.71), 122.13 (SD = 84.15), and 81.73 (SD = 49.44) in 2013, 2015, and 2017, respectively (see Table 2). The mean numbers of male high school students who carried handguns for the Democrat states were 129.44 (SD = 97.28), 125.57 (SD = 124.66), and 381.00 (SD = 568.80) in 2013, 2015, and 2017, respectively. The mean rates of male high school students who carried handguns for the Republican states were 0.140 (SD = 0.035), 0.145 (SD = 0.022), and 0.113 (SD = 0.031) in 2013, 2015, and 2017, respectively. The mean rates of male high school students who carried handguns for the Democrat states were 0.082 (SD = 0.023), 0.075 (SD = 0.026), and 0.080 (SD = 0.034) in 2013, 2015, and 2017 respectively.

Table 1. Sample Size Overview

Variable	Total number of observations	Number of states (%) per political party		Number of states per year		
		Republican	Democrat	2013	2015	2017
Males carrying guns	56	34 (60.7)	22 (39.3)	24	15	17

Table 2. Descriptive Statistics for the Variables of Interest

Variable	Year	Party	Number of states	Events		Trials		Events/Trials			
				M	SD	M	SD	M	SD	Min	Max
Male carrying guns	2013	R	15	109.53	83.71	760.67	465.30	0.140	0.035	0.099	0.207
		D	9	129.44	97.28	1469.11	977.53	0.082	0.023	0.049	0.112
	2015	R	8	122.13	84.15	806.63	444.49	0.145	0.022	0.105	0.172
		D	7	125.57	124.66	1537.29	1227.18	0.075	0.026	0.045	0.119
	2017	R	11	81.73	49.44	737.09	423.72	0.113	0.031	0.083	0.177
		D	6	381.00	568.80	4894.83	7516.20	0.080	0.034	0.042	0.138
	Overall	R	34	103.50	73.99	763.85	434.57	0.133	0.033	0.083	0.207
		D	22	196.82	313.70	2425.09	4079.49	0.079	0.026	0.042	0.138

Note: R = Republican; D = Democrat; M = mean; SD = standard deviation; Min = minimum; Max = maximum. Events represent the number of male high school students who carried handguns. Trials represent the male sample size. Events/Trials represent the rate of male high school students who carried handguns.

Figure 1 shows the bar chart of mean rates of males who carried handguns by year and political party, which provides a direct comparison of the mean rates of male high school students who carried handguns between the two political parties. Based on Figure 1, compared to Democrat states, Republican states seem to have higher mean rates of males who carry handguns. Indeed, the results of the logistic regression for repeated measures indicate that there is a statistically significant relationship between males who carry handguns and political party ($\chi 2(1) = 25.037$, $p < 0.001$, Table 3). In particular, males were 77.4% more likely to carry handguns in Republican states than in Democrat states (OR = 1.774, 95% CI = [1.417, 2.221], Table 4).

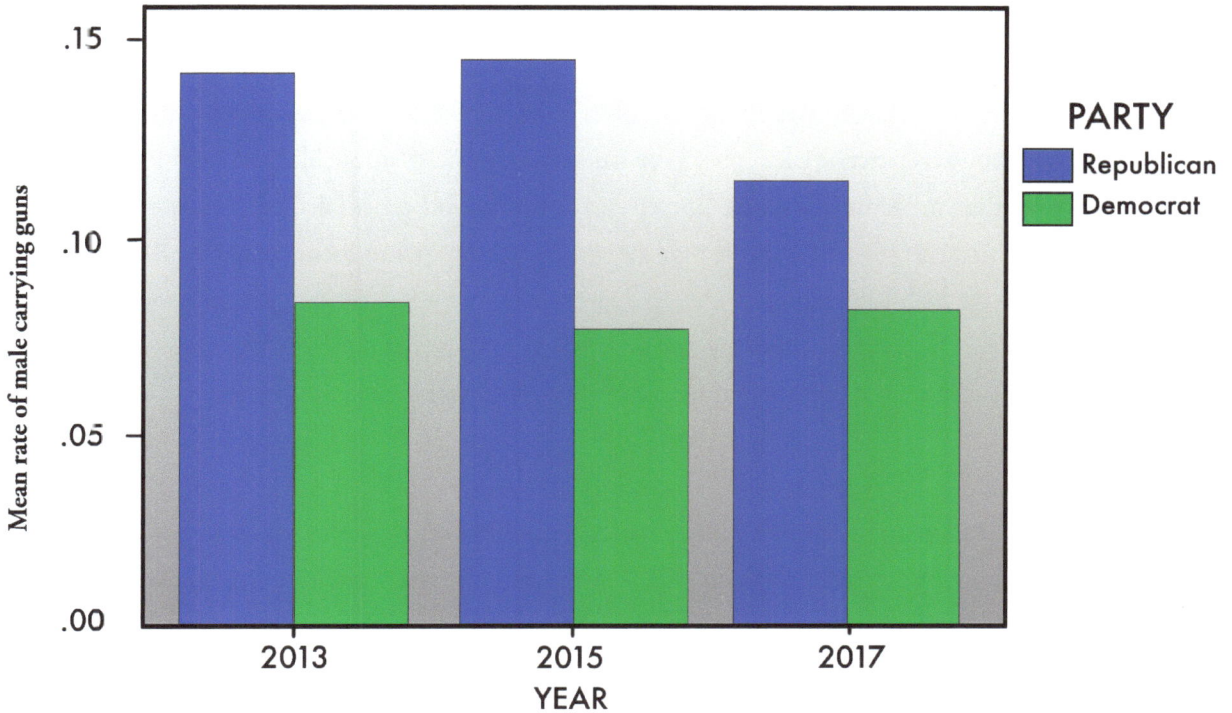

Figure 1. Bar chart of mean rates of male high school students who carried handguns by year and political party.

Table 3. Tests of Model Effects

Model	Wald χ^2	df	p
Male carrying guns	25.037	1	< 0.001

Note: Wald χ^2 = Wald chi-square statistic; df = degrees of freedom; p = p-value.

Table 4. Parameter Estimates and Odds Ratios

Model	Variable	B	SE	95% CI of B		OR	95% CI of OR	
				Lower	Upper		Lower	Upper
Male carrying guns	Intercept	-2.427	0.096	-2.614	-2.240			
	Political Party							
	Republican	0.573	0.115	0.349	0.798	1.774	1.417	2.221
	Democrat	Ref						

Note: B = parameter estimate; SE = standard error; CI = confidence interval; lower = lower bound; upper = upper bound; OR = odds ratio; ref = reference group. OR was computed as exp(B).

V. DISCUSSION

The results indicate that there is a statistically significant relationship between male high school students who carry handguns and political party. Male high school students were 77.4% more likely to carry handguns in Republican states than in Democrat states. Therefore, the null hypothesis is rejected. The results of this study are important because they may indicate that the social learning environment created by Republicans is more likely to encourage male high school students to carry handguns when compared to the social learning environment created by Democrats. Therefore, the problem of carrying handguns by high school students may be addressed through appropriate laws that create the proper social learning environment.

Limitations

There were several limitations in the current study. First, the extent of underreporting or overreporting of behaviors by the participants cannot be determined (Kann et al., 2016). Second, because the sample is limited to male high school students in the U.S., the findings cannot be generalized to other populations. Third, as stated earlier, the use of a nonparametric statistic may result in some loss of efficiency for the estimation of the coefficients relative to the use of a parametric statistic (Fitzmaurice et al., 2004; Su, 2020). Fourth, the differential association theory does not indicate whether pro-social or anti-social behaviors will be learned in any given environment (Siegel, 2018). In other words, two individuals exposed to the same social environment may learn two different behaviors. Fifth, because the study was quantitative in nature, it does not explain *why* male high school students carry handguns (Berg, 2007). Finally, social learning theorists dismiss biological factors and place too much emphasis on situational factors (Durkin, 1995). For example, social learning theorists fail to address the nature of human emotions. Indeed, they dismiss the notion that personality traits may be a major feature of social behavior.

REFERENCES

Berg, B.L. (2007). *Qualitative research methods for the social sciences* (6th ed.). Boston, MA: Pearson Education, Inc.

Davis, W.L. (2020). Is There a Difference Between Democrat and Republican States in the Number of Female Students Who Experienced Cyberbullying? *Lincoln Memorial Journal of Social Sciences, 1*(1), Article 1.

Duffin, E. (2020). *Number of law enforcement officers U.S. 2004-2019.* https://www.statista.com/statistics/191694/number-of-law-enforcement-officers-in-the-us/

Durkin, K. (1995). *Developmental social psychology: From infancy to old age.* Boston, MA: Blackwell.

Fitzmaurice, G. M., Laird, N. M., & Ware, J. H. (2004). *Applied longitudinal analysis.* Hoboken, NJ: John Wiley & Sons.

Gun Violence Achieve (2020). https://www.gunviolencearchive.org/past-tolls

Hatch, J. (2002). *Doing qualitative research in education settings.* Albany, NY: State University of New York.

Jehan, F., Pandit, V., O'Keeffe, T., Azim, A. Jain, A., Tai, S.A., Tang, A., Khan, M., Kulvatunyou, N., Gries, L., & Joseph, B. (2018). The burden of firearm violence in the United States: Stricter laws result in safer states. *Journal of Injury and Violence Research, 10*(1), 11-16. doi: 10.5249/jivr.v10i1.951

Kann, L., Kinchen, S., Shanklin, S.L., Flint, K.H., Hawkins, J., Harris, W.A., . . . Zaza, S. (2014). Youth risk behavior surveillance—United States, 2013. *Morbidity and Mortality Weekly Report: Surveillance Summaries, 63*(4), 1-172. https://www.cdc.gov/mmwr/pdf/ss/ss6304.pdf

Kann, L., McManus, T., Harris, W.A., Shanklin, S.L., Flint, K.H., Hawkins, . . . Zaza, S. (2016). Youth risk behavior surveillance—United States, 2015. *Morbidity and Mortality Weekly Report: Surveillance Summaries, 65*(6), 1-180. https://www.cdc.gov/healthyyouth/data/yrbs/pdf/2015/ss6506_updated.pdf

Kann, L., McManus, T., Harris, W.A., Shanklin, S.L., Flint, K.H., Hawkins, J., Queen, B., . . . Ethier, K.A. (2018). Youth risk behavior surveillance—United States, 2017. *Morbidity and Mortality Weekly Report: Surveillance Summaries, 67*(8), 1-479. https://www.cdc.gov/healthyyouth/data/yrbs/pdf/2017/ss6708.pdf

Khoshnood, A. (2019). Holding Sweden hostage: Firearm-related violence. *Forensic Sciences Research, 4*(1), 88-93.

Kleck, G., & Gertz, M. (1995). Armed Resistance to Crime: The Prevalence and Nature of Self-Defense with a Gun. *Journal of Criminal Law and Criminology, 86*(1), 150-187.

Lemieux, F. (2014). Effect of gun culture and firearm laws on gun violence and mass shootings in the United States: A multi-level quantitative analysis. *International Journal of Criminal Justice Sciences, 9*(1), 74-93.

Loftin, C., & McDowall, D. (1984). The deterrent effects of the Florida felony firearm law. *Journal of Criminal Law & Criminology, 75*(1), 250-259.

Lott, J.R., & Whitley, J.E. (2001). Safe-storage gun laws: Accidental deaths, suicides, and crime. *Journal of Law and Economics, 44*(S2), 659-689.

Ludwig, J. & Cook, P.J. (2000). Homicide and suicide rates associated with implementation of the Brady handgun violence prevention act. *JAMA, 284*(5), 585-591.

Pearson-Merkowitz, S., & Dyck, J.J. (2017). Crime and partisanship: How party ID muddles reality, perception, and policy attitudes on crime and guns. *Social Science Quarterly, 98*(2), 443-454. Doi: 10.1111/ssqu.12417

Presidential voting history by state (n.d.). https://ballotpedia.org/Presidential_voting_history_by_state

Rajan, S., Allegrante, J.P., Branas, & C.C., Hargarten, S. (2018). Funding for gun violence research is key to the health and safety of the nation. *American Journal of Public Health, 108*(2), 194-195. dci: 10.2105/AJPH.2017.304235

Siegel, L.J. (2018). *Criminology: Theories, patterns and typologies* (13th ed.). Boston, MA: Cengage.

Siegel, M., & Boine, C. (2019). *What are the most effective policies in reducing gun homicides?* Rockefeller Institute of Government. https://rockinst.org/wp-content/uploads/2019/08/8-13-19-Firearm-Laws-Homicide-Brief.pdf

Snyder, R.L. (2016). *The sport of politics simplified: Democrats versus Republicans, the 2016 Spectator's Guide.* Scotts Valley, CA: CreateSpace.

Su, Y. (2020). *Dr. Su Statistics.* https://sites.google.com/site/drsustat/

Thobaben, R.G., Schlagheck, D.M., & Funderburk, C. (1991). *Issues in American political life: Money, violence, and biology.* Englewood Cliffs, NJ: Prentice Hall.

United States Census Bureau (2020). *2020 demographic analysis.* https://www.census.gov/

Williams, F.P., & McShane, M.D. (2018). *Criminological theory* (7th ed.). New York, NY: Pearson.

Wright, J.D., & Rossi, P.H. (1985). *The Armed Criminal in America: A Survey of Incarcerated Felons.* National Institute of Justice, U.S. Department of Justice. https://www.ncjrs.gov/pdffiles1/photocopy/97099ncjrs.pdf

Political Partisanship and Female High School Students Who Carry Handguns

Trenton Cameron, Lincoln Memorial University (TN)
&
Wayne L. Davis, Ph.D., Columbia College (SC)

Abstract

The United States is a gun culture nation, and gun violence is a serious problem. Because there are more than 280 million guns in America with over 65 million handguns in circulation, the Republicans believe that there are too many guns in America to prevent criminals from illegally obtaining them. In addition, only law-abiding residents will honor gun-control laws. As a result, law-abiding residents will become defenseless, which will promote crime. Democrats, on the other hand, believe that the gun-related crime problem will never be solved until actions are taken to eliminate the availability of handguns. After all, it is hard to commit a gun-related crime if a person does not have the means to commit a gun-related crime. According to the Democrats, if the number of handguns in society is not reduced, then the gun-related crime problem will not be solved. According to the differential association theory, individuals become law violators when they are in contact with people, groups, and events that produce an excess of definitions that are favorable toward criminality. Criminal behaviors are influenced by the legal code and are learned via interactions with other people. Furthermore, a person's behavior will be influenced by the frequency, importance, duration, and intensity of the social learning experiences. By allowing or restricting the carrying of concealed handguns for law-abiding residents, Democrats and Republicans attempt to create the ambience they envision, which they believe will reduce social harm. If high school students carry concealed handguns, which is against the law, then this would indicate that they are learning to do so in that politically created social environment. Therefore, the purpose of this study was to determine if there is a difference between Democrat and Republican states in the percentage of female high school students who carry handguns in their respective jurisdictions. This study examined electronic second-hand data collected in 2013, 2015, and 2017 by the Centers for Disease Control and Prevention. Compared to Democrat states, Republican states seem to have higher mean rates of female high school students who carry handguns. However, the results of the logistic regression for repeated measures indicate that there is no statistically significant relationship between female high school students who carry handguns and political party. If either political party wants to demonstrate its superior gun-policy platform for female high school students, then it will need to do a better job at creating the proper ambience to address the problem.

I. INTRODUCTION

Political Partisanship & Gun-Related Attitudes

There is much political debate in the U.S. between Democrats and Republicans on handgun-control policies (Snyder, 2016). The United States is a gun culture nation, and gun violence is a serious problem (Goddard, 2011; Lott, 1998). There are more than 280 million guns in America with over 65 million handguns in circulation (Herbert, 2011; McGrory, 2006). As a result, the Republicans believe that there are too many guns in America to prevent criminals from illegally obtaining them. In addition, research has indicated that most of the homicides committed in Chicago, for example, are committed with old guns that have gone through a series of transactions (Siegel, 2018). In other words, newly purchased handguns obtained from registered gun dealers in documented sales are rarely used in crime. However, Democrats believe that the gun-related crime problem will never be solved until actions are taken to eliminate the availability of handguns. After all, it is hard to commit a gun-related crime if a person does not have the means to commit a gun-related crime. According to the Democrats, if the number of handguns in society is not reduced, then the gun-related crime problem will not be solved.

Firearm Threat

Firearms are a public safety issue that deserves further research. A 2018 poll conducted by the Pew Research Center indicates that 64% of juvenile girls and 51% of juvenile boys are worried that they may be shot at school (Idzikowski, 2020). This is understandable because there are about 300 people who are shot or killed every day in the U.S. on average (Goddard, 2011). Of these 300 individuals, 57 of them are juveniles. Of these 57 juveniles, nine of them die each day due to gun-related violence. Indeed, handguns are dangerous weapons. This is the reason why gun-carry laws have clauses in them that forbid guns to be carried into schools. If handguns were safe, then schools would not have been singled out.

Democrats

Democrats believe that gun-related crimes can be managed by controlling the social environment. Democrats support gun-control laws that restrict law-abiding individuals from carrying concealed handguns because they believe that the environment can be modified to change the behavior of potential criminals (Kirk, 2018; O'Connor, 2020; Snyder, 2016). Democrats believe that criminals are not totally responsible for their actions because they are a product of the social environment. If guns are removed from society, then criminals will have less access to them, thus, reducing gun-related crimes. In short, if the number of guns in society is reduced, then the number of gun-related crimes can be reduced.

Democrats also believe that civilians should not be able to take the law into their own hands because innocent persons may sometimes be hurt or killed (Snyder, 2016). Civilians are not trained to effectively enforce the law like police officers and, because they may personally be involved in the situation, they may be biased. For example, if two armed parties refuse to back down, and both believe they are right, this may result in a shooting. Police officers, on the other hand, are trained in the use-of-force, firearms, and verbal judo. Police officers are held liable for their bullets and know that deadly force can only be used in life-threatening situations (Del Carmen & Hemmens, 2017).

Republicans

Republicans oppose gun-control laws that restrict law-abiding adults from carrying concealed handguns because they feel that individuals have a right to protect their own lives whenever and wherever they believe they are threatened (Snyder, 2016). Republicans believe that disarming law-abiding civilians will enhance the violent crime problem because defenseless law-abiding citizens will become more attractive targets to the criminals. Indeed, criminals will come to learn that law-abiding civilians will not be armed. Republicans believe that criminals choose to commit acts of crime and a social environment filled with armed law-abiding residents will discourage crime (Siegel, 2018). If laws are passed to legally removed guns from society, then criminals will be the only ones who have access to them, which will increase gun-related crimes. After all, only law-abiding residents will honor gun-control laws, and law-abiding residents will become defenseless. In addition, gun-control laws will enhance the number of gun-related crimes because third party individuals who do not carry guns will lose the benefit gained from the criminals not knowing which individuals are carrying concealed weapons (Lott, 1998).

Law-abiding civilians who carry concealed handguns reduce the number of murders, rapes, and aggravated assaults (Lott, 1998). During many gun-related cases, the attacks are prevented by the law-abiding citizens simply brandishing their handguns. However, many of these cases are not reported to the authorities. Although about 30 people are accidental killed each year by private citizens who believed that they are protecting themselves, the police accidentally kill about 330 individuals per year. Relatively speaking, law-abiding civilians with guns are less dangerous than police officers with guns. Furthermore, arrestees have indicated during a survey that they were more afraid of armed victims than of police (Wright & Rossi, 1985).

Differential Association Theory

According to the differential association theory, individuals become law violators when they are in contact with people, groups, and events that produce an excess of definitions that are favorable toward criminality (Siegel, 2018). Criminal behaviors are influenced by the legal code and are learned via interactions with other people. Furthermore, a person's behavior will be influenced by the frequency, importance, duration, and intensity of the social learning experiences. By allowing or restricting the carrying of concealed handguns for law-abiding residents, Democrats and Republicans attempt to create the ambience they envision, which they believe will reduce social harm. If high school students carry concealed handguns, which is against the law, then this would indicate that they are learning to do so in that politically created social environment.

Public Safety and Research Question

Because there is disagreement between Democrats and Republicans about gun-control policies, and because the reduction of social harm is an important social goal, it is important to know if there is a difference between the jurisdictions of the two political parties in the gun-carrying practices of children. Therefore, the purpose of this study was to determine if there is a difference between political partisanship and the percentage of female high school students who carry handguns. The research question and the null hypothesis are listed below.

Research Question: Is there a difference between Democrat and Republican states in the percentage of female high school students who carry handguns?

Null Hypothesis: There is no difference between Democrat and Republican states in the percentage of female high school students who carry handguns.

II. LITERATURE REVIEW

First, DeSimone et al. (2013) conducted a study to investigate whether child access prevention laws are associated with decreased nonfatal gun injuries. Child access prevention laws hold the gun owner responsible if a child gains access to a gun that is not properly secured. Many of the prior research studies that investigated child access prevention laws have focused exclusively on gun-related deaths and not on gun-related injuries that were not fatal. To examine non-fatal gun injuries, the researchers examined data collected from annual hospital discharge records from 11 states for two age groups. One age group was comprised of individuals who were under 18 years of age and the other age group was comprised on individuals who were at least 18 years of age. The gun injury data were collected from the Agency for the Healthcare Research and Quality's Nationwide Inpatient Sample. To assess the data, the researchers employed Poisson regressions to control for various hospital, county, and state characteristics. The findings indicated that child access prevention laws were associated with reductions in nonfatal gun injuries among children under 18 years of age. These results were supported by the absence of self-inflicted injuries by weapons other than guns.

However, there were several limitations in the DeSimone et al. (2013) study. First, because data were only collected from 11 states, the findings cannot necessarily be generalized to states not considered in the study. Second, because the pre-intervention period was brief, there was little variation to exploit before the child access prevention laws were implemented. Finally, a quantitative study does not interpret each person's reality, does not explain *why* individuals behave in certain ways, and is ineffective for predicting human nature (Adams, 1999; Ponterotto, 2005).

Second, Crifasi et al. (2018) conducted a study to determine whether laws related to the sale, use, and carrying of firearms were related to homicide rates at the state level. Using an interrupted time series design, the researchers conducted a longitudinal study from 1984 to 2015 involving 136 large, urban counties in the U.S. To test for the effects of the laws, homicide was stratified by firearm versus all other methods, and Poisson regression was applied to account for national trends. The findings indicated that requiring a permit to purchase firearms was associated with decreased firearm homicide. In addition, the findings indicated that comprehensive background checks only, stand-your-ground laws, right-to-carry laws, and persons who were convicted of violent misdemeanors and possessed guns were all associated with increases in the number of firearm homicides.

However, there were several limitations in the Crifasi et al. (2018) study. First, there is a risk of selection bias, which may impact the validity of the findings. Only counties that had a population of 200,000 or more were considered in the study, and these counties may not necessarily reflect smaller counties. Second, information on law enforcement expenditures, which was a covariate in the study, was available at the state level but not at the county level. Finally, because the study was quantitative in nature, it investigated *how* variables were related (i.e., the method of operandi), but it did not investigate *why* the variables were related (i.e., the motive).

Third, Cheng and Hoekstra (2013) conducted a study to examine whether the enhancement of the castle doctrine, which promotes self-defense, deters crime. The enhancement of the castle doctrine included removing the duty to retreat in places outside of one's home and removing civil liability for those acting under the law. Data were collected on homicide, burglary, robbery, and aggravated assault across all 50 states from the Uniform Crime Report from 2000 to 2010. The researchers used a difference-in-differences regression framework to assess the data. The findings indicated that the enhancement of the castle law doctrine was positively related to the number of homicides. In addition, expansions to castle laws did not deter burglary, robbery, or aggravated assault. In short, the consequence of strengthening self-defense laws resulted in a net increase in homicides.

However, there were several limitations in the Cheng and Hoekstra (2013) study. First, some of the homicides could have been justifiable homicides. Thus, the homicide numbers used in the study may have been overexaggerate. Second, it is not possible to know the actual number of crimes committed in society because only about 40% of crimes are reported to the police (Berry & Smith, 2000; U.S. Department of Justice, 2010). Indeed, the FBI's Uniform Crime Report data differ from the U.S. Census Bureau's National Crime Victimization Survey data. Thus, crime statistics were incomplete and, consequently, they were less than accurate. Finally, the Uniform Crime Report data were determined by the number of arrests. Sometimes, innocent persons may be arrested. Thus, the crime statistics may be less than accurate.

Fourth, Marvell (2001) used a fixed-effects research design to assess the 1994 federal law that prohibits the possession of handguns by individuals under 18 years of age. State laws related to the ban of handguns were also evaluated. Data were collected from 1970 to 1999. Victimization data were collected from the Centers for Disease Control and Prevention, and juvenile victimization data were collected from the Bureau of Justice Statistics. Earlier total homicide data and gun homicide data were collected from mortality tables from the National Center for Health Statistics, Vital Statistics of the U.S. Finally, reported crime data were collected from the Uniform Crime Report. To assess the data, the researcher used multiple time-series regression with coefficient comparisons. The findings indicated that there was no significant relationship between banning firearms and the number of gun-related homicides.

However, there were several limitations in the Marvell (2001) study. First, state legislatures may have passed laws to ban guns in response to an increase in juvenile homicide. This will result in a misleading positive relationship between strict gun laws and the number of homicides. Second, data at the state level were incomplete and erratic, which may affect the validity of the study's findings. Finally, small states may have had no juvenile homicides in a given year. These states were disregarded during the data analysis because they create problems with regression analysis.

Finally, Rosengart et al. (2005) conducted a cross sectional time series study to determine if there was a relationship between state gun laws and firearm deaths. Data were collected from all 50 states and the District of Columbia from 1979 to 1998 from the National Center for Health Statistics. The five gun laws that were assessed were 1) shall issue laws that allow individuals to carry handguns unless restricted by other statutes, 2) age laws that prohibit individuals under 21 years of age to purchase handguns, 3) age laws that prohibit individuals under 21 years of age to possess handguns, 4) frequency laws that prohibit individuals from buying more than one gun per month, and 5) junk gun laws that ban cheaply constructed handguns. To assess the data, the researchers used Poisson regression to determine mortality rate ratios. As a result, the findings indicated that there was no significant relationship between the gun laws and the number of firearm homicides or firearm suicides.

However, there were several limitations in the Rosengart et al. (2005) study. First, the study's analysis was restricted to states that had passed at least one of the five laws under study. If smaller jurisdictions within the states had passed similar laws before the statewide laws were enacted, then the study's findings may have underestimated any effect. Second, if city or county ordinances passed similar laws after the statewide laws were enacted, then the researchers may have measured the effect of the local ordinances instead of the state law. Finally, because the study was a quantitative study, it does not interpret each person's reality and is ineffective for predicting human nature (Adams, 1999; Ponterotto, 2005).

In sum, the studies are mixed. On the one hand, some studies indicate that handguns and stand-your-ground laws promote social harm. These studies seem to support strong gun-control policies. On the other hand, some studies challenge the effectiveness of gun-control policies. According to these studies, gun control polices have failed to serve their purpose, and law-abiding citizens may need to protect themselves. It is difficult to say how the ambience created by each political party may impact the behaviors of female high school students.

III. METHODOLOGY

Political Partisanship Definition

A state was considered either Democrat or Republican based on the political party of the state governor during the years of data collection, which were 2013, 2015, and 2017 ("List of Governors of the American States," n.d.). If a state's governor belonged to the Democrat party from the beginning of 2013 till the end of 2017, then that state was considered a Democrat state. If a state's governor belonged to the Republican party from the beginning of 2013 till the end of 2017, then that state was considered a Republican state. To be considered in this study, a state had to be consistently Democrat or Republican during all years of data collection.

Data

Data were collected by the Centers for Disease Control and Prevention in 2013, 2015, and 2017 using the Youth Risk Behavior Surveillance System (Kann et al., 2014; Kann et al., 2016; Kann et al., 2018). The standard questionnaire in 2013 included 86 questions, and the standard questionnaires in 2015 and 2017 included 89 questions. A three-stage cluster sample of female high school students, who attended public and private schools, produced a nationally representative sample of female students in grades 9-12.

Statistical Analysis

Because data were collected every two years from the same states, and students typically attend high school for four years, there is a possibility that the same students responded to more than one survey. Indeed a prior study that used Poisson regression on the same data source has indicated that there is correlation among the data values, which resulted in a huge overdisperson problem (Davis, 2020). To address this parametric statistic assumption violation, the current study used a generalized estimating equation (GEE), which is a nonparametric statistic, to assess the data. However, nonparametric statistics are not as strong as parametric statistics (Field, 2005). In other words, relative to the use of a parametric statistic, the use of a nonparametric statistic, such as GEE, may result in some loss of efficiency for the estimation of the coefficients (Fitzmaurice et al., 2004; Su, 2020).

IV. RESULTS

Data were collected from 18 states in 2013, 13 states in 2015, and 13 states in 2017 for a total of 44 observations (see Table 1). Of all the states considered, 75% were Republican and 25% were Democrat. The mean numbers of female high school students who carried handguns for the Republican states were 22.79 (SD = 18.45), 29.67 (SD = 28.44), and 21.00 (SD = 23.91) in 2013, 2015, and 2017, respectively (see Table 2). The mean numbers of female high school students who carried handguns for the Democrat states were 44.75 (SD = 30.07), 38.00 (SD = 35.73), and 46.33 (SD = 35.81) in 2013, 2015, and 2017, respectively. The mean rates of female high school students who carried handguns for the Republican states were 0.026 (SD = 0.012), 0.034 (SD = 0.014), and 0.025 (SD = 0.010) in 2013, 2015, and 2017, respectively. The mean rates of female high school students who carried handguns for the Democrat states were 0.025 (SD = 0.009), 0.020 (SD = 0.017), and 0.021 (SD = 0.014) in 2013, 2015, and 2017, respectively.

Table 1. Sample Size Overview

Variable	Total number of observations	Number of states (%) per political party		Number of states per year		
		Republican	Democrat	2013	2015	2017
Females who carried handguns	44	33 (75.0)	11 (25.0)	18	13	13

Table 2. Descriptive Statistics for the Variables of Interest

Variable	Year	Party	Number of states	Events		Trials		Events/Trials			
				M	SD	M	SD	M	SD	Min	Max
Females who carried handguns	2013	R	14	22.79	18.45	818.07	449.27	0.026	0.012	0.008	0.050
		D	4	44.75	30.07	1831.75	1189.39	0.025	0.009	0.016	0.037
	2015	R	9	29.67	28.44	870.56	800.81	0.034	0.014	0.016	0.069
		D	4	38.00	35.73	1686.25	1238.84	0.020	0.017	0.007	0.044
	2017	R	10	21.00	23.91	747.00	452.27	0.025	0.010	0.016	0.044
		D	3	46.33	35.81	2017.67	1587.66	0.021	0.014	0.009	0.037
	Overall	R	33	24.12	22.67	810.85	549.68	0.028	0.012	0.008	0.069
		D	11	42.73	30.42	1829.55	1186.50	0.022	0.012	0.007	0.044

Note: R = Republican; D = Democrat; M = mean; SD = standard deviation; Min = minimum; Max = maximum. Events represent the number of female high school students who carried handguns. Trials represent the female sample size. Events/Trials represent the rate of female high school students who carried handguns.

Figure 1 shows the bar chart of mean rates of females who carried handguns by year and political party, which provides a direct comparison of the mean rates of female high school students who carried handguns between the two political parties. Based on Figure 1, compared to Democrat states, Republican states seem to have higher mean rates of female high school students who carry handguns. However, the results of the logistic regression for repeated measures indicate that there is no statistically significant relationship between female high school students who carry handguns and political party ($\chi2(1) = 0.959$, $p = 0.327$, Table 3; OR = 1.282, 95% CI = [0.780, 2.109], Tables 4).

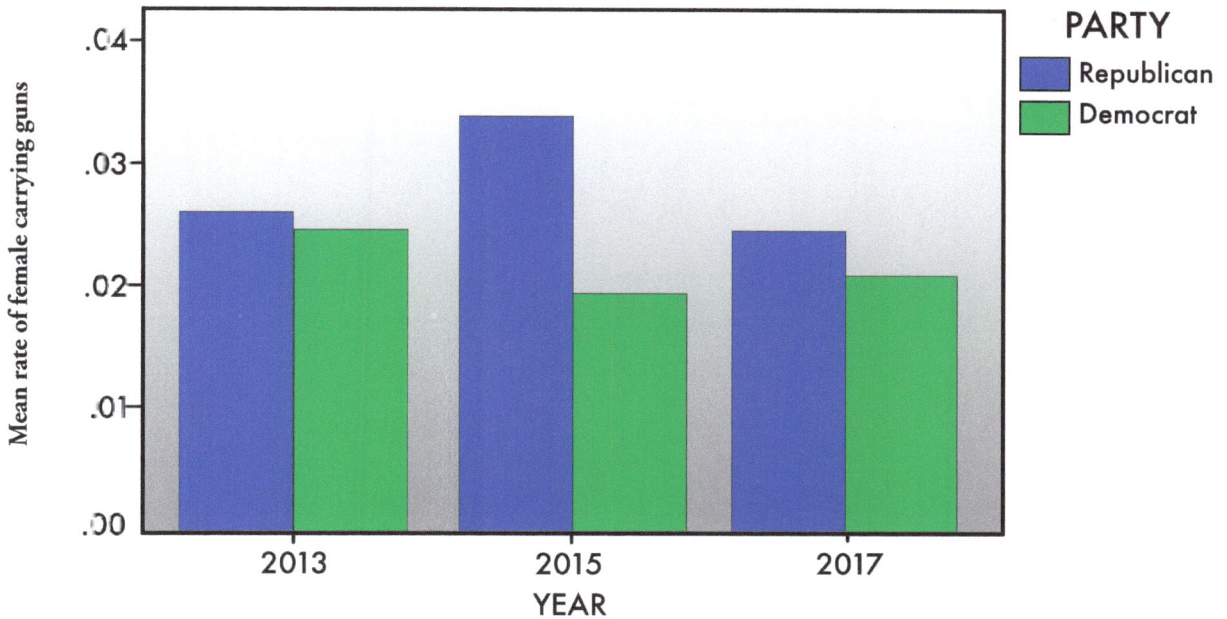

Figure 1. **Bar chart of mean rates of female high school students who carried handguns by year and political party.**

Table 3. **Tests of Model Effects**			
Model	Wald $\chi2$	df	p
Females who carried handguns	0.959	1	0.327

Note: Wald $\chi2$ = Wald chi-square statistic; df = degrees of freedom; p = p-value.

Table 4. **Parameter Estimates and Odds Ratios**								
Model	Variable	B	SE	95% CI of B		OR	95% CI of OR	
				Lower	Upper		Lower	Upper
Females who carried handguns	Intercept	-3.733	0.231	-4.187	-3.280			
	Political Party							
	Republican	0.249	0.254	-0.249	0.746	1.282	0.780	2.109
	Democrat	Ref						

Note: B = parameter estimate; SE = standard error; CI = confidence interval; lower = lower bound; upper = upper bound; OR = odds ratio; ref = reference group. OR was computed as exp(B).

V. DISCUSSION

Compared to Democrat states, Republican states seem to have higher mean rates of female high school students who carry handguns. However, the results of the logistic regression for repeated measures indicate that there is no statistically significant relationship between female high school students who carry handguns and political party. Therefore, the null hypothesis is accepted. This study is important because it demonstrates that neither political party is better than the other when it comes to creating a social learning environment that discourages female high school students from carrying handguns. If either political party wants to demonstrate its superior gun-policy platform for female high school students, then it will need to do a better job at creating the proper ambience to address the problem.

Limitations

There were several limitations in this study. First, because the sample was limited to female high school students in grades 9-12, the findings cannot be generalized to other populations. Second, because of the study was not based on an experimental design, it cannot determine causal relationships. Third, although social learning theorists believe that exterior forces influence interior behavior, they fail to consider cognitive development (Durkin, 1995). Fourth, because the study was quantitative in nature, it does not explain *why* female high school students carry or do not carry handguns (Berg, 2007). Fifth, because Likert-type scales were used during the collection of the data, there is a possibility that the participants may have simply selected positive responses over negative responses (Antonovich, 2008). Finally, there are different ways to define political partisanship, which may provide different results. For example, political partisanship may be defined by the political party affiliation of a state's Senate or House of Representatives.

REFERENCES

Adams, W. (1999). The interpermeation of self and world: Empirical research, existential phenomenology, and transpersonal psychology. *Journal of Phenomenological Psychology, 30*(2), 39-55.

Antonovich, M.P. (2008). *Office and SharePoint 2007 user's guide: Integrating SharePoint with Excel, Outlook, Access, and Word.* Berkeley, CA: Apress.

Berg, B.L. (2007). *Qualitative research methods for the social sciences* (6th ed.). Boston, MA: Pearson Education, Inc.

Berry, B., & Smith, E. (2000). Race, sport, and crime: The misrepresentation of African Americans in team sports and crime. *Sociology of Sport Journal, 17*(2), 171-197.

Cheng, C. & Hoekstra, M. (2013). Does strengthening self-defense law deter crime or escalate violence? Evidence from expansions to Castle Doctrine. *The Journal of Human Resources, 48*(3), 821-853.

Crifasi. C.K., , Merrill-Francis, M., McCourt, A., Vernick, J.S., Wintemute, G.J., Webster, D.W. (2018). Association between Firearm Laws and Homicide in Urban Counties. *Journal of Urban Health, 95*(3):383-390. doi: 10.1007/s11524-018-0273-3.

Davis, W.L. (2020). Is There a Difference Between Democrat and Republican States in the Number of Female Students Who Experienced Cyberbullying? *Lincoln Memorial Journal of Social Sciences, 1*(1), Article 1.

Del Carmen, R.V. & Hemmens, C. (2017). *Criminal procedures: Laws & practice* (10th ed.). Boston, MA: Cengage.

DeSimore, J., Markowitz, S., & Xu, J. (2013). Child Access Prevention Laws and Nonfatal Gun Injuries. *Southern Economic Journal, 80* (1), 5-25.

Durkin, K. (1995). *Developmental social psychology: From infancy to old age.* Boston, MA: Blackwell.

Field, A. (2005). *Discovering statistics using SPSS* (2nd ed.). Thousand Oaks, CA: Sage.

Fitzmaurice, G. M., Laird, N. M., & Ware, J. H. (2004). *Applied longitudinal analysis.* Hoboken, NJ: John Wiley & Sons.

Goddard, A. (2011). Gun violence is a serious problem. In L.I. Gerdes (Ed.), *Gun violence: Opposing viewpoints* (p. 25-29). Farmington Hills, MI: Greenhaven Press.

Herbert, B. (2011). The availability of guns increases gun violence. In L.I. Gerdes (Ed.), *Gun violence: Opposing viewpoints* (p. 85-89). Farmington Hills, MI: Greenhaven Press.

Idzikowski, L. (2020). Introduction. In L. Idzikowski (Ed.), *School shootings: Introducing issues with opposing viewpoints* (p. 7-9). New York, NY: Greenhaven Publishing.

Kann, L., Kinchen, S., Shanklin, S.L., Flint, K.H., Hawkins, J., Harris, W.A., . . . Zaza, S. (2014). Youth risk behavior surveillance—United States, 2013. *Morbidity and Mortality Weekly Report: Surveillance Summaries, 63*(4), 1-172. https://www.cdc.gov/mmwr/pdf/ss/ss6304.pdf

Kann, L., McManus, T., Harris, W.A., Shanklin, S.L., Flint, K.H., Hawkins, . . . Zaza, S. (2016). Youth risk behavior surveillance—United States, 2015. *Morbidity and Mortality Weekly Report: Surveillance Summaries, 65*(6), 1-180. https://www.cdc.gov/healthyyouth/data/yrbs/pdf/2015/ss6506_updated.pdf

Kann, L., McManus, T., Harris, W.A., Shanklin, S.L., Flint, K.H., Hawkins, J., Queen, B., . . . Ethier, K.A. (2018). Youth risk behavior surveillance—United States, 2017. *Morbidity and Mortality Weekly Report: Surveillance Summaries, 67*(8), 1-479. https://www.cdc.gov/healthyyouth/data/yrbs/pdf/2017/ss6708.pdf

Kirk, C. (2018). *10 things Democrats will take away from us if they win control of the House and Senate.* https://www.foxnews.com/opinion/10-things-democrats-will-take-away-from-us-if-they-win-control-of-the-house-and-senate

List of governors of the American states (n.d.). https://ballotpedia.org/List_of_governors_of_the_American_states

Lott, J.R. (1998). More guns, less crime: *Understanding crime and gun-control laws.* Chicago, IL: University of Chicago Press.

Marvell, T.B. (2001). The impact of banning juvenile gun possession. *Journal of Law and Economics, 44*(S2), 691-713.

McGrory, M. (2006). Guns are to blame for school shootings. In S. Barbour (Ed.), *Writing the critical essay: School violence. Opposing viewpoints guide* (p. 18-23). Farmington Hills, MI: Greenhaven Press.

O'Connor, L. (2020). *5 Big Government, America-Destroying Schemes Democrats are Proposing During COVID-19 Crisis.* https://townhall.com/columnists/larryoconnor/2020/03/17/5-big-government-americadestroying-schemes-democrats-proposed-during-covid19-crisis-n2565105

Ponterotto, J. (2005). Qualitative research in counseling psychology: A primer on research paradigms and philosophy of science. *Journal of Counseling, 52*(2), 126-136.

Rosengart, M., Cummings, P., Nathens, A., Heagerty, P., Maier, R., & Rivara, F. (2005). An evaluation of state firearm regulations and homicide and suicide death rates. *Injury Prevention, 11*(2), 77-83.

Siegel, L.J. (2018). *Criminology: Theories, patterns and typologies* (13th ed.). Boston, MA: Cengage.

Snyder, R.L. (2016). *The sport of politics simplified: Democrats versus Republicans, the 2016 Spectator's Guide.* Scotts Valley, CA: CreateSpace.

Su, Y. (2020). *Dr. Su Statistics.* https://sites.google.com/site/drsustat/

U.S. Department of Justice, Office of Justice Programs, Bureau of Justice Statistics (2010). *Criminal victimization in the United States, 2007 statistical tables: National crime victimization survey.* http://bjs.ojp.usdoj.gov/content/pub/pdf/cvus0705.pdf

Wright, J.D., & Rossi, P.H. (1985). *The Armed Criminal in America: A Survey of Incarcerated Felons.* National Institute of Justice, U.S. Department of Justice. https://www.ncjrs.gov/pdffiles1/photocopy/97099ncjrs.pdf

www.ingramcontent.com/pod-product-compliance
Lightning Source LLC
Chambersburg PA
CBHW041542260326
41914CB00015B/1528